SAMUEL JOHNSON
ON SHAKESPEARE

SAMUEL JOHNSON
ON SHAKESPEARE

EDITED, WITH AN INTRODUCTION BY

W. K. WIMSATT, JR.

A DRAMABOOK
HILL AND WANG · NEW YORK

Et J. C. W.
OLIM LEGENDUM

CONTENTS

INTRODUCTION

I

Let us begin by looking at a certain few scenes or moments from the externally narratable career of Samuel Johnson.

And first, one which occurs in the late winter of 1737 —the place, anywhere along the road between Lichfield, in Staffordshire, and London. Two men are making their way to the metropolis—by what means the record does not quite make clear, but perhaps partly on foot, partly on horseback. The older man, son of a poor bookseller in Lichfield, a one-time resident at Oxford but not a graduate, and latterly master of a small boys' academy near his native town, is now in his twenty-eighth year— a large, bony, and ungainly figure as he moves along, wearing his own hair, parted behind, straight and stiff, over a face scarred by childhood disease, and gray eyes, wild and piercing, though he is nearsighted. Perhaps he is now and then given to "convulsive starts and odd gesticulations." This is of course Samuel Johnson. The younger man, twenty years old, a smaller, trimmer and more agile figure, no doubt more dapper, is also a resident of Lichfield, has been not long ago one of the very few pupils at Johnson's academy. He is on his way now as an equal and companion-at-arms for the trial of fortune in London. Between them they carry in their pockets, as they would much later recall in jest, "two-pence half-penny," and "three half-pence." Johnson brings with him also an unfinished tragedy entitled *Irene*. At the moment when this scene occurs, there is nothing actually remarkable about it for the history of Shakespearian criticism and appreciation. But sentimentally and with the benefit of our retrospective piety, we may say that there is. For these two men will, between them, though in quite different ways, during the next forty years do more than any other persons in England to usher in a new era in Shakespearianism. The second man is David Garrick.

After his arrival in London Garrick, thinking to become a lawyer but soon discovering that he *was* in fact an actor, worked very hard and rose fast, making a reputation in his first Shakespearian role, Richard III, in 1741 at the Goodman's Field Theater. And so our second scene takes place only ten years after the first, on September 15, 1747, when Garrick, who had become a joint owner and the manager of the Drury Lane Theater, inaugurated his management with a production of Shakespeare's *Merchant of Venice*. This scene, so far as it is available to us, consists mostly in the words of a *Prologue* which Johnson wrote, presumably at Garrick's request, and which Garrick recited.

> When Learning's triumph o'er her barbarous foes
> First reared the stage, immortal Shakespeare rose.
>
> The wits of Charles found easier ways to fame,
> Nor wished for Jonson's art or Shakespeare's flame.
>
> Perhaps where Lear has raved and Hamlet died,
> On flying cars new sorcerers may ride.
>
> 'Tis yours this night to bid the reign commence
> Of rescued Nature and reviving Sense.

The poem is a kind of "progress piece" in reverse, celebrating the decline of the English stage from the time of Shakespeare to the recent reign of pantomime, song, and farce. Shakespeare is involved by name in only three passages, altogether twelve lines of the poem's total sixty-two. Yet in a very real sense, only somewhat spread out in generalizations, Shakespeare is the subject of this poem. Here we have the united voices of Johnson and Garrick in the announcement of a view about dramatic art and a program with which all the rest of Johnson's critical career and Garrick's theatrical career were to be concerned—though sometimes, as we shall see, in less than perfect harmony.

A third important moment in our series occurs many years later. In fact, one of its distinctive features, almost a notorious feature, is the extraordinary delay which occurred between its first promise and the achievement. Let us run rapidly over certain data: and first the fact that in January 1744 Garrick had made one of his most notable contributions to the growth of the Shakespearian theater, when he had the original and bold idea of bringing on at Drury Lane the complete or nearly complete text, unexpurgated and unaltered, of Shakespeare's *Macbeth* ("as Shakespeare wrote it"). Garrick's life record in respect to the rendering of Shakespeare was an excellent one—though it is true that he would later not have the courage to restore the Fool in *Lear* or the unhappy ending (1756), and he would be guilty of the ruthless amputation of the gravediggers in *Hamlet* (1772). Back in 1744, Garrick in restoring the text of *Macbeth* had perhaps had the advantage of some editorial work which had already been done by Samuel Johnson.[1] For it was about the same time, or in April 1745, that Johnson first issued a set of proposals for an edition, in ten volumes, decimo octavo, of the "plays" of Shakespeare, and backing up these proposals, printed along with them as a cover or container a specimen of a Shakespeare commentary, a small book entitled *Miscellaneous Observations on the Tragedy of Macbeth*. This proposal was the promise which, for various reasons in succession, was to take so long in the maturing. Aside from initial obstacles of copyright, Johnson encountered for about fifteen years many other, more immediately pressing, claims on his time: for example, his *Dictionary of the English Language*, on historical principles, published in 1755 (after eight years of sustained labor), the *Rambler* essays (208 in number, from 1750 to 1752), and then the *Adventurer* essays, the *Idler* essays, and during the same period as the last, *Rasselas* (1759). Nevertheless, in June 1756, or about a year after he was quit of the *Dictionary,* Johnson issued a new set of *Proposals* for Shakespeare—a short and trenchant essay, in effect, on the duties of a Shakespeare editor. But Johnson was by now rapidly settling into the posture of a successful literary man of middle age. In 1762 he received a pension of £300 a year. This was the time when he began to fold his legs and to sit back and enjoy both the bread and tea of life and the turtle and burgundy. Several times he thought, or hoped, that he would finish Shakespeare within the next few months. The satirist Charles Churchill wrote some couplets that have become immortal in the manner of the grubs in amber alluded to by Pope.

[1] See George Winchester Stone, Jr., "Garrick's Handling of *Macbeth*," *Studies in Philology*, XXXVIII (October 1941), 609–628; "Garrick's Production of *King Lear*," *Studies in Philology,* XLV (January 1948), 89–103; "Garrick's Long Lost Alteration of *Hamlet*," *PMLA*, XLIX (September 1934), 890–921.

He for subscribers baits his hook,
And takes their cash, but where's the book?
No matter where; wise fear, we know,
Forbids the robbing of a foe.
But what, to serve our private ends,
Forbids the cheating of our friends?

Spurred on perhaps by this attack and perhaps roused too by some sort of wager which his friends are said to have contrived, Johnson did at length finish his Shakespeare. The edition appeared in October 1765, eight volumes in octavo, the text of the plays, with Johnson's weighty annotations throughout (added to many from the earlier editors) and in the first volume his incomparable *Preface*. We may form a sufficient image of this edition for the moment and place it in the history of Shakespeare scholarship if we remark that this was the sixth "research" edition, or more or less learned yet popular editing, of Shakespeare to appear, the first having been that of the dramatic poet Nicholas Rowe in the year of Johnson's birth (1709), which had been followed by the antithetic editions—the appreciative and free versus the scholarly and careful—of Pope (1726) and Theobald (1734), and then by the editions of Sir Thomas Hanmer (1744) and of William Warburton (1747). Hanmer's Oxford edition was remarkable for its magnificent printing [1] and Warburton's edition for the license of his conjectures in emendation. Nicholas Rowe's *Account of the Life of Mr. William Shakespeare*, which had appeared in his edition, was still the standard life, and Pope's rearrangement of it was printed by Johnson in his first volume, along with the *Prefaces* of all his predecessors. Johnson's grand edition was destined to be reprinted frequently during the next sixty years. With the corrections and amplifications contributed by George Steevens (1773, 1778), Edmond Malone (1780), Isaac Reed (1785), and the younger James Boswell (1821), Johnson's work evolved into a variorum edition which was the climax and summation of the eighteenth-century tradition in Shakespeare editing. "Boswell's

---

[1] Hanmer's edition had come out just in time for Johnson in 1745 to add to his *Observations on Macbeth* a section of *Remarks on Sir T.H.'s Edition of Shakespeare*. "Surely the weapons of criticism ought not to be blunted against an editor who can imagine that he is restoring poetry while he is amusing himself with alterations like these. . . ."

Malone," the twenty-one-volume variorum of 1821, is still, as David Nichol Smith says (with perhaps only a slight exaggeration), "the standard complete edition" of Shakespeare.

A fourth and last moment in Johnson's career at which we shall look is not the same sort of public moment in the history of letters. In a sense it may be called an anticlimax. It occurs eight years after the publication of Johnson's *Shakespeare*—eleven years before the death of Johnson and a little more than five years before the death of Garrick—in the late summer of 1773. Once more, two men are traveling together. This time they are Johnson and his much younger friend James Boswell. They are in a post chaise driving along the northern coast of Scotland, through the shire of Murray on their way to the Hebrides. They come during an afternoon to the "very heath" (as they suppose or allow themselves to suppose) "where Macbeth met the witches. Dr. Johnson . . . solemnly repeated—

> How far is't call'd to Forres? What are these,
> So wither'd, and so wild in their attire?"

"He repeated a good deal more of *Macbeth*. His recitation was grand and affecting. He then parodied the *All-hail* of the witches to Macbeth," addressing himself to Boswell, who had recently purchased a new estate. Johnson "condescended to amuse himself with uttering:

> All hail Dalblair! hail to thee, Laird of Auchinleck!" [1]

We will call it a part of the same scene when the next morning, as they resumed their journey and even before stopping at the next town for breakfast, Boswell asked Johnson one of his favorite questions: Why had he not mentioned Garrick in his *Preface* to Shakespeare? Johnson answered:

I would not disgrace my page with a player. Garrick has been liberally paid for mouthing Shakespeare. If I should praise him, I should much more praise the nation who paid him. He has not made Shakespeare better known. He cannot illustrate Shakespeare. He does not understand him. Besides, Garrick got me no subscriptions. He did not furnish me with his old plays.

[1] Pronounced "Affleck."

I asked to have them, and I think he sent me one. It was not worth while to ask again.[1]

This is laughable. It is also sad. Even here, even in the golden realm of letters, of Shakespearian study and appreciation, Johnson and Garrick were experiencing one of the forms of mortality which we might hope would be one of the least inevitable, but which in fact the irritable race of literary men all too often do experience— the strange alteration of old friendship. Two chief complaints stood against his old pupil and traveling companion Davy: one that as a mere actor of Shakespeare he really didn't amount to much—"a poor player, who frets and struts his hour upon the stage,"—"a shadow." [2] The other: that Garrick had held back from lending old copies of plays for collation. The second topic might be amusingly enough elaborated from the anecdotal history of the times.[3] The first is deeply entangled in more theoretical issues which have a stronger claim on our attention. One of the sturdiest of all intellectual critics in the Aristotelian tradition, Johnson was capable of expressing a "heterodox . . . contempt" not only of Garrick but of tragic acting in general. "He said, 'The action of all players in tragedy is bad. It should be a man's study to repress those signs of emotion and passion.' " [4] In his *Preface* he delivers the dictum: "A play read affects the mind like a play acted."

[1] From *Boswell's Journal of a Tour to the Hebrides with Samuel Johnson, LL.D.,* ed. Frederick A. Pottle and Charles H. Bennett (New York, 1936), p. 207, September 23, 1773. Reprinted by permission of Yale University and McGraw-Hill Book Company, Inc.

[2] *Life,* II, 92, October 19, 1769.

[3] Garrick had complained to Boswell about a covert phrase in Johnson's *Preface:* "I collated such copies as I could procure, and wished for more, but have not found the collectors of these rarities very communicative." Garrick's version of the affair was that he had left the key of his library "with a servant, with orders to have a fire and every convenience for him." But Johnson had apparently wanted to be courted more actively. Boswell observes that "considering the slovenly and careless manner in which books were treated by Johnson, it could not be expected that scarce and valuable editions should have been lent him" (*Life,* II, 192, Spring 1772).

[4] *Life,* V, 38, August 15, 1773.

II

It is true that Shakespeare was more or less regularly acted all through the eighteenth century. Every great actor from Betterton to Kean, observes David Nichol Smith, made his name by acting Shakespeare. Even so far back as the year of *The Beggar's Opera* (1728) the ordinary playgoer could have seen ten different Shakespeare plays. But in the year of *She Stoops to Conquer* (1773) he could have seen fifteen.[1] A brisk upswing in Shakespearian theater during the mid-century was to a considerable extent the work of Garrick. After he took over at Drury Lane in 1747 Garrick averaged no fewer than forty-four performances of Shakespeare annually until his retirement in 1776, and in the course of his career he produced twenty-eight different Shakespearian plays, and he himself assumed eighteen Shakespearian roles. And Garrick's acting texts had the merit, on the whole, of giving the audience less and less of "Shakespeare improved," more and more of the real Shakespeare.[2] "Had not the plays of Shakespeare lain dormant for many years before the appearance of Mr. Garrick? Did he not exhibit the most excellent of them frequently for thirty years together, and render them extremely popular by his own inimitable performance?" Years later, in a note to the third edition of his *Tour to the Hebrides*, Boswell undertook to explain what Johnson "must necessarily have meant" when he said that Garrick could not "illustrate" Shakespeare. Johnson must have meant that:

Mr. Garrick did not as *a critic* make Shakespeare better known; he did not *illustrate* any one *passage* in any one of his plays

[1] Smith, 1928, pp. 25–26.
[2] George Winchester Stone, Jr., "David Garrick's Significance in the History of Shakespearean Criticism," *PMLA,* LXV (March 1950), 183–197; "The God of His Idolatry, Garrick's Theory of Acting and Dramatic Composition with Especial Reference to Shakespeare," *Joseph Quincy Adams Memorial Studies* (Washington, 1948), p. 128. Stone takes his figures in both articles from the Winston Manuscript *Dramatic Register,* 1700–1803, in the Folger Shakespeare Library. During a bad decade when pantomimes reigned (1750–1760), a total of 527 performances, or 30% of the Drury Lane production, went to Shakespeare (*Adams Studies,* p. 117).

by acuteness of disquisition or sagacity of conjecture; and what had been done with any degree of excellence in *that* way was the proper and immediate subject of his preface.[1]

The extravagant, somewhat vulgar Shakespeare Jubilee at Stratford in September 1769, staged by Garrick and attended by Boswell in the character of a Corsican Chief, might be adduced to illustrate what Garrick was doing for the popular reputation of Shakespeare. On the other hand—and it may be more difficult for us today, after two centuries of the Shakespeare industry, to realize this—Shakespeare in the world of scholars and critics, the sober world of paper and argument, was still partly lacking in advancement. The old prestige of Ben Jonson as the learned and correct dramatic poet which G. E. Bentley has in our day shown to have outrun the prestige of Shakespeare through the greater part of the seventeenth century,[2] might still enjoy at least ghostly, or facetious, echoes. Samuel Johnson's 1747 *Drury Lane Prologue* tells us how Shakespeare the *natural* poet was at that date outstripping Jonson the *learned* and artful. The mere persistence of such a contrast, however, argues that there was still something left for Shakespeare to gain. Johnson in that *Prologue* was in fact defining an area where he himself had a special role to play. Bringing to his task as editor his own already vast prestige as lexicographer, poet, and moral essayist, Johnson was in a position to confer some benefits on Shakespeare. In spite of the liberties of adverse criticism which he took, or perhaps, as Boswell believed, partly because of such liberties,[3] Johnson succeeded in giving a strong push to the process by which Shakespeare was soon to become an unimpeachable figure. Johnson with his edition and Garrick with

[1] Stone, *PMLA* March 1950, especially pp. 184, 195, shows that a considerable segment of Garrick's audience, including Johnson's collaborator George Steevens, did find Garrick's acting an excellent "commentary" upon Shakespeare, an "elucidation" of difficult passages.

[2] Gerald Eades Bentley, *Shakespeare & Johnson, Their Reputations in the Seventeenth Century Compared* (Chicago, 1945), I, 138–140.

[3] "We must confess the faults of our favorite, to gain credit to our praise of his excellencies" (Johnson to Charles Burney, October 16, 1765). Sherbo, p. 56, believes that Johnson was actually more restrained than other critics in finding fault with Shakespeare, though his judgment was more independent.

his Jubilee are the joint initiators of that phase of our literary history which is known today as "The Genesis of Shakespeare Idolatry" or "The Grass Roots of Bard-olatry." [1]

III

Certain generally received opinions concerning Johnson's achievement as a Shakespeare editor would appear to be substantially correct. Let us attempt a brief recital. Johnson entertained very sound views about the philological part of an editor's duties. His performance in this respect was, by modern standards, uneven, capricious, often notably deficient. But by any standards illustrated up to his own day, his performance was extraordinary. For reasons in part no doubt well shown in the relation with Garrick which we have noticed, Johnson did only a spotty job in the department of textual collation. At the same time, he restored many readings of the First Folio and was the first editor to realize its sole authority among the folios. In the department of explication, or, as it was then called, "elucidation," of the difficult passages in Shakespeare, Johnson relied for the most part on his own sturdy good sense and general awareness of human nature, but now and then he made good use too of the historical perspectives which he had learned in his *Dictionary* labors and in which he had great confidence and took a justifiable pride.[2] He wrote a number of notes which were repeated by Shakespearian editors until at least as recently as the Furness *Variorum* volumes and which perhaps still deserve to be repeated more often than they are. Perhaps the largest philological virtue which Johnson displayed was that of restraint in the department of emendation, humility in the face of his author's text, respect for what was given. He was much less classically squeamish, he was less confident in, or hopeful for, any kind of rational purity, than most of his predecessors. ("It has been my settled principle that a reading of the ancient books is probably true." "I have adopted the Ro-

[1] R. W. Babcock, *The Genesis of Shakespeare Idolatry, 1766–1799,* Chapel Hill, 1931; Martha Winburn England, "The Grass Roots of Bardolatry," *Bulletin of the New York Public Library,* LXIII (March 1959), 117–133.
[2] See below, p. 20.

man sentiment, that it is more honorable to save a citizen than to kill an enemy.")

In one other department of philology, his performance was deficient almost to the degree of scandal. During the long years of the promise and the waiting, he had encouraged one of his protégées, the American lady novelist Charlotte Ramsay Lennox, in a very ambitious undertaking. Her book entitled *Shakespeare Illustrated,* three volumes, published in 1753 and 1754, was an inquiry which went far beyond the earlier efforts of Langbaine, Gildon,[1] and Theobald in actually *studying* the source books for Shakespeare's stories. The Dedication to the Earl of Orrery which Johnson wrote for Mrs. Lennox, taken in conjunction with the book itself, is a kind of milepost in the contemporary movement away from neoclassic norms of appreciation. Johnson is perhaps the first English critic to utter an explicit and emphatic commitment against the ancient tradition of objectivity in the established story and to voice a regret (or at least to *threaten* [2] a regret) that Shakespeare in respect to his plots was not more original or inventive. At the same time Johnson entertained plans, or at least in his *Proposals* he soon uttered promises, to make great use of Shakespeare's sources when he came to his own editing. The fact, however, is that he did rather little in this way. Johnson seems to have been not really very much interested in Shakespeare's sources.[3] We cannot

[1] Gerard Langbaine, *An Account of the English Dramatic Poets,* Oxford, 1691, *lists* the sources of twenty-seven Shakespeare plays. Charles Gildon's revision of Langbaine in 1698, *The Lives and Characters of the English Dramatic Poets,* makes a few additions. Mrs. Lennox *presents the text* (or a translation) of the sources of twenty-two Shakespeare plays and undertakes some analysis of his way of using them. See Young, pp. 151, 181–183.

[2] The first half of this curiously balanced or self-canceling critical document argues that the most important thing to know about an author is the degree of originality in his plot. The second half assures us that Shakespeare's merits are of a different order. See also Johnson's remarks on originality in the *Preface,* below, pp. 43–47.

[3] He refers to *Shakespeare Illustrated* by its title three times —in connection with the sources of *All's Well That Ends Well, Measure for Measure,* and *The Winter's Tale.* He seems to have consulted the same work, though he does not mention it, in connection with *The Two Gentlemen of Verona, Romeo and Juliet, King Lear,* and in general the English-history plays. See Young, pp. 204–220.

of course condone this deficiency. We may, however, let it go some way in our minds to make the remarks concerning originality in the *Dedication* for Mrs. Lennox look only momentary and nugatory.

IV

Let us turn now to Johnson's considered critical estimate of Shakespeare, and especially to the *Preface*. There are two main things that need to be said. First, there is the fairly simple but resounding sense in which Johnson rises to his occasion and succeeds not only in formulating a general praise, or encomium, but in lifting this a few degrees above the level of the already eloquent tradition. Ben Jonson had made the first announcement in his poem in the First Folio, "To the Memory of My Beloved, The Author Mr. William Shakespeare." Dryden in his *Essay of Dramatic Poesy* had demonstrated the idiom in prose. Shakespeare, wrote Dryden, "was the man, who, of all modern and perhaps ancient poets, had the largest and most comprehensive soul. All the images of nature were still present to him, and he drew them not laboriously, but luckily: When he describes any thing, you more than see it, you feel it too. . . ."

Johnson quotes this passage of Dryden's at the end of his *Preface* to Shakespeare. (In his *Life of Dryden* he was to allude to it as "a perpetual model of encomiastic criticism.") He has opened his own *Preface*, however, not precisely in the manner of Dryden, but at his own pace, with his own series of majestic commonplaces, stately hyperboles.

The poet of whose works I have undertaken the revision may now begin to assume the dignity of an ancient and claim the privilege of established fame and prescriptive veneration.

Nothing can please many, and please long, but just representations of general nature.

Shakespeare is above all writers, at least above all modern writers, the poet of nature, the poet that holds up to his readers a faithful mirror of manners and of life.

In the writings of other poets a character is too often an individual; in those of Shakespeare it is commonly a species.

His real power is not shown in the splendor of particular

passages, but by the progress of the fable and the tenor of his dialogue; and he that tries to recommend him by select quotations will succeed like the pedant in Hierocles, who, when he offered his house to sale, carried a brick in his pocket as a specimen.

Shakespeare has no heroes; his scenes are occupied only by men.

The other main thing to be said about Johnson's critical estimate of Shakespeare is this: that Johnson was an outright dissenter against the neoclassic rules and proprieties which had for long inhibited, and still did to some degree inhibit, the full appreciation of Shakespeare, the free response to his mystery.

It *is* a noteworthy fact that this freedom on the part of Johnson was rather severely limited as he encountered the immediate surface of Shakespeare's work—either individual scenes of certain sorts or the turns of dialogue, the rhetorical elaborations, the play of words—what today we should call the verbal texture. The several pages near the beginning of Johnson's *Preface* in which he lists and animadverts upon Shakespeare's "faults" or "defects" are not likely to be favorite pages with the modern critic. Shakespeare "makes no just distribution of good or evil"—"He omits opportunities of instructing or delighting"—he is guilty of anachronisms—in his comic scenes his "jests are commonly gross" and his "pleasantry licentious"—in his tragedies he runs into "tumor, meanness, tediousness, and obscurity."

[He] no sooner begins to move than he counteracts himself; and terror and pity, as they are rising in the mind, are checked and blasted by sudden frigidity.

A quibble is to Shakespeare what luminous vapors are to the traveller; he follows it at all adventures. . . . A quibble, poor and barren as it is, . . . was to him the fatal Cleopatra for which he lost the world and was content to lose it.

But Johnson's response to Shakespeare was, as we have already noted, not like that of the pedant in Hierocles who carried a brick in his pocket as a specimen of a house. Not the "splendor of particular passages" but the whole "progress of the fable and the tenor" of the "dialogue" was what he found irresistible in Shakespeare. Just how this division in Johnson's appreciation was pos-

sible—how he got to the heart of Shakespeare—perceived
the progress and tenor of the drama—except through the
aesthetic surface, the particulars of actions and words,
may be difficult to understand. Doubtless we confront
here some incompleteness of conversion, an unresolved
tension between the neoclassic conscience and the liberat-
ing impulse. Johnson the lexicographer would of course be
most painfully sensitive to the jaggedness of the verbal
idiom—the maverick particularities.

Johnson's defense of Shakespeare's irregularities, his
Gothicism, takes place in respect to broad principles of
dramatic structure—principles which neoclassic critics (Rymer, for instance, or even Dryden in his more Gallic
phase) had been just as much inclined to censure as the
licentious diction. A simpler and more obvious part of
this defense, one that may not have required much real
daring on Johnson's part, concerns the celebrated neo-
Aristotelian—no doubt pseudo-Aristotelian—unities of time
and place. The most careful American scholars have in
recent years been making a point of denying Johnson any
credit for this—it was like kicking open a door that had
for many years been standing ajar. Johnson's arguments
can be found a century earlier in the prefaces of Dryden's opponent Sir Robert Howard, or at the turn of
the century in Farquhar's *Discourse upon Comedy,* or
more strikingly, in very similar terms, in Lord Kames's
Elements of Criticism, published only three years ahead
of Johnson's *Preface.*[1] I think the answer is that, although
doubtless neither the French-Italian ideas nor the rebuttal
of them were any longer novel—still the issue was not
dead. Johnson at least pretended to be afraid of formidable opposition: "I am almost frighted at my own temerity and, when I estimate the fame and the strength of
those that maintain the contrary opinion, am ready
to sink down in reverential silence." [2] What is even more
to the point, Johnson deserves credit for meeting this
issue in a characteristic display of two of his most valu-

[1] Thomas M. Raysor, "The Downfall of the Three Unities,"
Modern Language Notes, XLII (1927), 1–9; Sherbo, pp. 57–59.
[2] Smith, 1928, p. 75, notes that Johnson had contributed to
a translated work by Mrs. Lennox, *The Greek Theater of Father
Brumoy,* 3 vols., 1759, and thinks that in his discussion of the
unities Johnson is answering the "Discourse upon the Original
of Tragedy" in vol. I, pp. xliii–xlvi.

able powers. For one thing, he goes immediately to the heart of the matter, putting his finger on the false premise by which the exaggerated doctrine of the unities had so long been sustained—namely, the assumption that the aim of drama is literal verisimilitude, "the supposed necessity of making the drama credible." For another thing, even if he is only kicking an open door, he does this with such ample energy and gusto, such resonance, reverberation of splintering material, that it is doubtful if carpenters will be able very soon to mend this door.

The objection . . . supposes that when the play opens the spectator really imagines himself at Alexandria and believes that his walk to the theater has been a voyage to Egypt, and that he lives in the days of Antony and Cleopatra. Surely he that imagines this may imagine more. He that can take the stage at one time for the palace of the Ptolemies may take it in half an hour for the promontory of Actium. Delusion, if delusion be admitted, has no certain limitation; if the spectator can be once persuaded that his old acquaintance are Alexander and Caesar, that a room illuminated with candles is the plain of Pharsalia or the bank of Granicus, he is in a state of elevation above the reach of reason.

The truth is that the spectators are always in their senses and know, from the first act to the last, that the stage is only a stage and that the players are only players.

Time is, of all modes of existence, most obsequious to the imagination.

The delight of tragedy proceeds from our consciousness of fiction; if we thought murders and treasons real, they would please no more.

Whether Shakespeare knew the unities and rejected them by design, or deviated from them by happy ignorance, it is, I think, impossible to decide and useless to inquire.

A second heading under which Johnson is to be ranked as a liberal defender of Shakespeare is both more difficult to define and more important than the first. Under this head Johnson himself seems far from being as certain and clear as he is about the unities. And here too we encounter a special point of interest in the fact that one of Johnson's opponents was Voltaire. Despite the well-known racy pessimism, or "realism," of such a work as his *Candide* (a *roman* in which he had for a moment in 1759 paralleled the mood of the English moralist, in his *Rasselas*), Voltaire subscribed to a fairly exalted version of the neoclassic proprieties. He very often observed gross blemishes in Shakespeare. He thought of Shakespeare as a "genius" who had not a "spark" of good taste and not the slightest knowledge of the laws of art.[1] In his *Appel à toutes les Nations* (1761) and perhaps in some other place, not yet identified by the scholars, Voltaire had recently risked some observations which get appropriate echoes in Johnson's *Preface*.[2]

Dennis and Rymer think . . . [Shakespeare's] Romans not sufficiently Roman; and Voltaire censures his kings as not completely royal. Dennis is offended that Menenius, a senator of Rome, should play the buffoon; and Voltaire perhaps thinks decency violated when the Danish usurper is represented as a drunkard. But Shakespeare always makes nature predominate over accident. . . . He knew that Rome, like every other city, had men of all dispositions; and wanting a buffoon, he went into the senate house for that which the senate house would certainly have afforded him. He was inclined to show an usurper and a murderer not only odious, but despicable; he therefore added drunkenness to his other qualities, knowing that kings love wine like other men, and that wine exerts its natural power upon kings.

This passage comes just at the end of Johnson's praise of Shakespeare as the poet of general truth to human nature. But the argument, with the examples invited by Dennis, Rymer, and Voltaire, has brought Johnson to the threshold of something much more difficult. Is general human nature pure, or impure? Or is it each by turns? —or both at once? And what, on any one of these suppositions, are the appropriate feelings? Within a few pages, as we have already noticed, Johnson will be complaining that in Shakespeare's plays "terror and pity, as they are rising in the mind, are checked and blasted by sudden frigidity." But now, with Voltaire and the drunken Danish usurper, Dennis and the senatorial buffoon, in good focus, with the whole "progress" and "tenor" of plays doubtless in mind, Johnson proceeds at his next step into a wider arena and announces that he will undertake to defend Shakespeare against the time-honored objection that he "mixes his comic and tragic scenes." More than a dozen years earlier, in the *Rambler*, Johnson had

---

[1] See Voltaire's *Lettres sur les Anglais,* 1734, *Lettre* XVIII.
[2] See below, pp. 28, 31, 44.

touched on this Shakespearian theme, using a key phrase which he now uses again, "mingled drama." His restatement now (though surely perplexed and in part undercut if we read it in the context of the later censures which we have quoted) is for the moment energetic, earnest, and profound. It must surely be one of the few most pregnant passages of dramatic criticism written in England during the eighteenth century.

Shakespeare's plays are not in the rigorous and critical sense either tragedies or comedies, but compositions of a distinct kind; exhibiting the real state of sublunary nature, which partakes of good and evil, joy and sorrow, mingled with endless variety of proportion and innumerable modes of combination; and expressing the course of the world, in which the loss of one is the gain of another; in which, at the same time, the reveller is hasting to his wine, and the mourner burying his friend; in which the malignity of one is sometimes defeated by the frolic of another; and many mischiefs and many benefits are done and hindered without design.

Shakespeare has united the powers of exciting laughter and sorrow not only in one mind but in one composition.

That this is a practice contrary to all the rules of criticism will be readily allowed; but there is always an appeal open from criticism to nature.

v

Let us proceed to a conclusion by taking some notice of certain motions of Johnson's spirit which may be conceived as not entirely subdued to the schemes of his critical reasoning. One difference between Johnson and most other literary critics, and especially between him and many other critics of his own time, is the fullness and depth with which he responds to a work of literature and to the author of that work. Johnson responds with a massive movement of his personality. Sometimes this works to inform and illuminate a critical judgment, as in the intuition which we have just seen, that Shakespeare's "mingled drama" is an artistically right exhibition of the "real state of sublunary nature." At other times, we are likely to feel that a statement of Johnson's is not so much an act of theoretical intelligence as a direct confrontation of one personality with another. The more massive this other personality, and the more opposite to

Johnson's, the more memorable the statement may be: Milton is perhaps the most signal instance. "His political notions were those of an acrimonious and surly republican." "His family consisted of women, and there appears in his books something like a Turkish contempt of females." The distinctly antithetic though slighter personality of Johnson's contemporary, the poet Gray, affords another instance. "Sir, he was dull in company, dull in his closet, dull everywhere. He was dull in a new way, and that made many people think him GREAT. He was a mechanical poet." [1]

One very general result of the entrance of Johnson's personality into his criticism is that even his most reasoned and dispassionate utterances almost always sound very much like the man we have sat with in the back parlor of Tom Davies's or walked with in the Hebrides. The resemblance between Johnson's conversation and his moral essays was often noticed by his friends. It extends even into what we might think the most unlikely places. The shortest note in the Shakespeare edition is likely to seem a characteristic shove of the shoulder by the Great Cham.

I know not how the ladies will approve of the facility with which both Rosalind and Celia give away their hearts.

I cannot reconcile my heart to Bertram.

But Falstaff, unimitated, unimitable Falstaff, how shall I describe thee?

For the obsequies of Fidele, a song was written by my unhappy friend Mr. William Collins of Chichester.

The enumeration of the choughs and crows . . . peoples the desert of intermediate vacuity.

[Polonius] is subject to sudden dereliction of his faculties.

This speech . . . is too horrible to be read or to be uttered. (*Hamlet*, III. iii. 94)

I am glad that I have ended my revisal of this dreadful scene. It is not to be endured. (*Othello*, V. ii)

This direct, personal, and conversational quality of Johnson's critical utterance ought not to be too readily taken for granted. Consider, for instance, the *difference* between the conversation or the epistolary style of the

[1] See W. Powell Jones, "Johnson and Gray: A Study in Literary Antagonism," *Modern Philology*, LVI (May 1959), 243–253.

Scotch hanging judge Lord Kames ("Friend Boswell, I have not been much accustomed to answer casuistical queries. . . . Take what you have got for your peeping.") [1]—the difference between this and the measured analytical tread of the associationist philosopher in his *Elements of Criticism.* Or consider the difference between Boswell himself having tea with Johnson and Mrs. Williams and Boswell expounding the nature of comedy in his *Hypochondriack* or writing *Observations . . . on Squire Foote's . . . Minor.*

Johnson's personality can be seen in his Shakespeare editing in a number of ways that are perhaps merely amusing. The student of literary criticism will no doubt be satisfied with a fairly brief allusion to Johnson's numerous retorts and rebukes, his tart dismissals of the previous editors, his solemn astonishment at their vanity and their bungling. ("A commentator naturally wishes to reject what he cannot understand.") [2] Johnson expresses his admiration of some of the editors in his *Preface,* and he declares a kind of general amnesty. Nevertheless he has his joke at their expense often enough in the course of the eight volumes. His strokes at Warburton were so impolite that he decided at the last moment to hold up publication and cancel some of them.[3] But this is not the confrontation of Johnson's personality with that of Shakespeare.

And again, the critic will perhaps not wish to linger long with the fairly numerous and diverse curiosities, the bric-a-brac, of Johnson's commentary—his notes on the mandrake root, the jewelled toad, the glowworm's

[1] Lord Kames to Boswell, October 13, 1770, in *Boswell for the Defence 1769–1774,* ed. William K. Wimsatt, Jr. and Frederick A. Pottle (New York: McGraw-Hill Book Company, Inc., 1959), p. 24.

[2] *All's Well That Ends Well,* I. i. 179. "*Batch* is changed by Theobald to *botch,* and the change is justified by a pompous note" (*Troilus and Cressida,* V. i. 5). "There is no end of such alterations; every page of a vehement and negligent writer will afford opportunities. . . . Dr. Warburton will have the devil *fiery,* because he makes the day *hot;* the author makes him *airy,* because *he hovers in the sky*" (*King John,* III. ii. 1–3). ". . . nor would Shakespeare now thank the officiousness of his editors, who restore what they do not understand" (*King Lear,* I. iii.19).

[3] A. T. Hazen, "Johnson's Shakespeare, a Study in Cancellation," *Times Literary Supplement,* December 24, 1938, p. 820.

eyes, the serpent's tongue, his repeatedly raised eye-brow at the horns of cuckoldry. Surely one of the strangest errors in the history of criticism appears in his note on the tailor in *King John* who in a hurry thrusts his slippers upon contrary feet.

Shakespeare seems to have confounded a man's shoes with his gloves. He that is frighted or hurried may put his hand into the wrong glove, but either shoe will equally admit either foot. The author seems to be disturbed by the disorder which he describes.

To a lady who once inquired of Johnson how it happened that he had a wrong definition of the word "pastern" in his *Dictionary*, it is well known that he gave the un-varnished reply: "Ignorance, Madam, pure ignorance." Such an answer concerning the foot of a horse no doubt compels acceptance. But our imagination may well balk at the attempt to conceive what Johnson would have said had this matter of the indifferent shoes ever been forced upon his attention.

That note of course is an unparalleled demonstration of philosophic detachment, rather than an instance of response with the whole personality. But to return to our serious theme: There is a part of one of Johnson's notes to Shakespeare which above all deserves quotation. This is the well-known passage on Cordelia in the General Observation on *King Lear*.

Shakespeare has suffered the virtue of Cordelia to perish in a just cause, contrary to the natural ideas of justice, to the hope of the reader, and, what is yet more strange, to the faith of chronicles. . . . A play in which the wicked prosper and the virtuous miscarry may doubtless be good, because it is a just representation of the common events of human life; but since all reasonable beings naturally love justice, I cannot easily be persuaded that the observation of justice makes a play worse, or that, if other excellencies are equal, the audience will not always rise better pleased from the final triumph of persecuted virtue.

In the present case the public has decided. Cordelia, from the time of Tate, has always retired with victory and felicity. And, if my sensations could add anything to the general suffrage, I might relate, I was many years ago so shocked by Cordelia's death that I know not whether I ever endured to read again the last scenes of the play till I undertook to revise them as an editor.

Now this passage, so directly and eloquently expressive of Johnson's feelings (or his "sensations"), and along with this many other places in the notes, some of which we have quoted a few pages back, do not sit in the easiest kind of relation to that notable defense of mingled or incongruous feelings which appears in the *Preface*. Johnson is a man of powerful and spontaneous responses to Shakespearian drama, but it is apparently not just these responses, or not these responses in their purest, simplest or most immediate shape, that give him his theoretical, his reasoned, his cerebrated defense of Shakespeare's adulterations. Johnson's emotional responses are more like the standard ones of his time; they are fairly close to the theoretical neoclassic norm, to the ideal of rational orderliness, the contemporary spirit of optimism and benevolism. This might be taken to mean that Johnson's defense of mingled drama was a mere abstract and thin cerebration which for some reason he undertook in opposition to his own genuine responses. But perhaps not. It is difficult to imagine any external reason which could have coerced him. The defense of mingled drama is indeed a testimony to Johnson's theoretical intelligence, but at the same time it would seem to be tied into something very deep, though sometimes less articulate and clear, in Johnson's nature—that is, his strongly religious sense of mystery in the universe, of the inscrutable—the supernatural. This sense, when it is operating, induces in him a much less demanding attitude toward the terrestrial distribution of good and evil, rewards and punishments. It is this sense largely which moves the Johnson who wrote the pleasantly darkened fable of *Rasselas*, the Johnson who turned his withering scorn on the complacent rationalism of Soame Jenyns's *Free Inquiry into the Nature and Origin of Evil*.

What is the earliest anecdote we have concerning Johnson on Shakespeare? "When he was about nine years old," says Mrs. Piozzi, "having got the play of *Hamlet* in his hand, and reading it quietly in his father's kitchen, he kept on steadily enough, till coming to the ghost scene, he suddenly hurried upstairs to the street door that he might see people about him." What are the later, even the latest anecdotes? How stood it between Shakespeare and Johnson as he grew into old age? "For many years," says Arthur Murphy, "when . . . [Johnson] was not disposed to enter into the conversation going forward, whoever sat near his chair might hear him repeating . . .

> Ay, but to die, and go we know not where;
> To lie in cold obstruction and to rot. . . ."

And Boswell gives us the following last word:

About eight or ten days before his death, when Dr. Brocklesby paid him his morning visit, he seemed very low and desponding and said, "I have been as a dying man all night." He then emphatically broke out in the words of Shakespeare:—

> Canst thou not minister to a mind diseas'd,
> Pluck from the memory a rooted sorrow . . . ?

To which Dr. Brocklesby readily answered:

>   Therein the patient
> Must minister to himself.

Johnson expressed himself much satisfied with the application.

Here we have a response to Shakespeare in the most direct, the least theoretical fashion. No doubt we learn more about Johnson in such confrontations than about Shakespeare. These are instances of a sort which cannot readily be adduced either to clarify or to justify Johnson's literary theory or criticism. These instances do, however, tell us something about Johnson the man, and they may suggest a reason in the depths for some of the failures of perfect alignment (and some of the most brilliant moments of success) on the surface of Johnson's account of Shakespeare. Although Johnson has long enjoyed a reputation as the last of the neoclassic giants, there is an established trend among learned readers of Johnson today to see his classicism as a thing very much altered from the Augustan norm. In his confrontation of Shakespeare especially, we discover Johnson to be far from the perfect neoclassic critic, and, in a much deeper sense, far from the representative illuminato of that day.

ACKNOWLEDGMENTS

Though the vehicle is slender, I should first like to pay a tribute to the memory of Karl Young, who was my instructor in a Yale graduate seminar in Shakespeare and Shakespearian criticism during the spring term of 1937, and who was the author of a monograph entitled *Samuel Johnson on Shakespeare, One Aspect*, which is still one of the best introductions to the whole subject.

Let me at the same time name and thank four of my own pupils in a seminar in the Age of Johnson—George Farr, Bell Gale, Robert F. Irving, and Katharine T. Jobes—who during the spring term of 1959 prepared for my use timely reports on the several duties and opportunities of an editor of Johnson on Shakespeare. In the same class, Roger J. Porter annotated a series of *Ramblers* which included the two in this volume.

Five of my associates in work on the Yale Edition of Samuel Johnson, Walter Jackson Bate, Allen T. Hazen, Frederick W. Hilles, Herman W. Liebert, and Albrecht B. Strauss, have contributed in various ways, sometimes without being aware of it, to the shaping of this little volume, and especially to the editing of the *Ramblers*. See below, p. 4.

In matters of Shakespeare scholarship I turned for advise to my colleague Charles T. Prouty.

A very substantial acknowledgment of a different kind is due to my helper on a Yale Bursary Appointment, Charles S. Swartz, Class of 1961, who typed the entire text of the selections from Johnson and performed numerous jobs of both textual and topical research. The book would not have been put together during the fall term of 1959 without his very able assistance.

In the Bibliography which follows and in notes throughout the book, I have indicated the main authorities whose ideas and information I have used. Let me add here a general acknowledgment of debt to the accumulation of notes for Johnson's *Preface* which begins with David Nichol Smith's *Shakespeare in the Eighteenth Century*, 1903, and continues in C. H. Conley's *Reader's Johnson*, 1940, and Bertrand Bronson's *Samuel Johnson*, 1952–1958.

It may be appropriate to say something about the relation of the present volume to Sir Walter Raleigh's *Johnson on Shakespeare*, Oxford, 1908, 1925 (revised). I have included three short texts which are not in Raleigh: the Drury Lane *Prologue,* the *Dedication* for Mrs. Lennox, and *Rambler* 156; like Raleigh, I present the *Proposals* of 1756, the *Preface* of 1765, and *Rambler* 168. Raleigh's book is longer than mine because he includes more than twice as many pages of the 1765 *Notes.* My principle of selection will be understood from a passage of my Introduction (p. xxvi) and from my editorial comment on the *Notes* (p. 70). I include a few *Notes* which are not in Raleigh; some of these were added in the Johnson-Steevens edition of 1773. Raleigh's Introduction is perhaps echoed here and there in my own, though the structure is basically different.

W. K. Wimsatt, Jr.

Yale University
January 30, 1960

SELECTED BIBLIOGRAPHY

Boswell, James, *The Life of Samuel Johnson, LL.D.*, G. B. Hill and L. F. Powell, eds., 6 vols., Oxford, 1934–1950.

Courtney, William Prideaux, *A Bibliography of Samuel Johnson, Revised and Seen through the Press by David Nichol Smith*, Oxford, 1915.

Krutch, Joseph Wood, *Samuel Johnson*, New York, 1944: Chapter IX, "Shakespeare."

Rowe, Nicholas, *Some Account of the Life of Mr. William Shakespeare* (1709), with an Introduction by Samuel H. Monk, Augustan Reprint Society, Extra Series, No. 1, 1948.

Sherbo, Arthur, ed., *Johnson's Notes to Shakespeare*, Augustan Reprint Society Publications, Nos. 59, 60, 65, 66, 71, 72, 73, 1956–1958. [The Johnson-Steevens text of 1773. A useful reprint.]

————, *Samuel Johnson Editor of Shakespeare*, Illinois Studies in Language and Literature, vol. 42, Urbana, 1956. [Close analysis of Johnson's relation to earlier Shakespeare scholarship and of his revisions of his editing in 1773 and later.]

Smith, David Nichol, *Shakespeare in the Eighteenth Century*, Oxford, 1928. [Three lectures, on theater, scholarship, criticism.]

Stone, George Winchester, Jr., "David Garrick's Significance in the History of Shakespearean Criticism," *PMLA*, LXV (March 1950), 183–197. [Other articles in an important series by Stone on Garrick and Shakespeare are cited in notes to my Introduction.]

Theobald, Lewis, *Preface to the Works of Shakespeare* (1734), with an Introduction by Hugh G. Dick, Augustan Reprint Society Publication No. 20 (Extra Series, No. 2), Los Angeles, 1949.

Young, Karl, *Samuel Johnson on Shakespeare, One Aspect*, University of Wisconsin Studies in Language and Literature No. 18 (Madison, 1924), pp. 147–227. [On Johnson and Mrs. Charlotte Ramsay Lennox but includes a general survey of Johnson on Shakespeare.]

Further bibliographical information will be found in notes at various places in this volume. A number of the works included in this list are cited in the notes by the name of the author and will be easily identified by reference to the list.

NOTE ON THE TEXT

The text adopted is that of first editions—except for the *Ramblers* and the *Notes* on *Macbeth*. See the footnotes attached to the titles. But here and there, especially in the *Preface* and *Notes* of 1765, a number of significant later readings have been introduced and are duly noted.

The spelling, hyphenation, and capitalization have been normalized to conform to G. & C. Merriam Company's *Webster's Collegiate Dictionary*, 1936. Certain instances of initial capitalization, in both verse and prose passages, are not typical of modern usage but have been retained to support a degree of personification in the sense.

Quotation marks, rather than the italics of Johnson's printed texts, have been used for longer quotations, and italics have been removed from set-off verse quotations, but have been retained in quotations of shorter phrases and single words, whether of prose or verse.

The punctuation has been somewhat altered (chiefly but not entirely by the *omission* of commas and *reduction* of semicolons) to conform to modern usage relating to clauses in a series and to the difference between restrictive and nonrestrictive clauses and phrases. The eighteenth-century punctuation of Johnson's texts is, however, very intimately related to the peculiarities of his rhetoric and syntax. His elaborately parallel, elliptical, and often suspended structures cannot be completely repunctuated by modern rules without being often very much obscured.

The spelling and punctuation of Shakespeare quotations throughout have been modernized according to W. J. Craig's Oxford text of 1930.

SAMUEL JOHNSON
ON SHAKESPEARE

PROLOGUE [1747]

Spoken by Mr. Garrick
At the Opening of the Theater in Drury Lane 1747 [1]

When Learning's triumph o'er her barbarous foes
First reared the stage, immortal Shakespeare rose;
Each change of many-colored life he drew,
Exhausted worlds, and then imagined new;
Existence saw him spurn her bounded reign,
And panting Time toiled after him in vain;
His powerful strokes presiding truth impressed,
And unresisted passion stormed the breast.

Then Jonson came, instructed from the school,
To please in method and invent by rule;
His studious patience and laborious art
By regular approach essayed the heart;
Cold Approbation gave the lingering bays,
For those who durst not censure scarce could praise,
A mortal born he met the general doom,
But left, like Egypt's kings, a lasting tomb.

The wits of Charles found easier ways to fame,
Nor wished for Jonson's art or Shakespeare's flame;
Themselves they studied; as they felt, they writ;
Intrigue was plot, obscenity was wit.
Vice always found a sympathetic friend;
They pleased their age and did not aim to mend.
Yet bards like these aspired to lasting praise
And proudly hoped to pimp in future days.
Their cause was general, their supports were strong,
Their slaves were willing, and their reign was long;
Till Shame regained the post that Sense betrayed,
And Virtue called Oblivion to her aid.

[1] The text follows the first edition, *Prologue Spoken by Mr. Garrick at the Opening of the Theater in Drury Lane 1747*, London, Printed by E. Cave at St. John's Gate . . . 1747 (Facsimile, New York, 1902). See also *The Poems of Samuel Johnson*, ed. D. Nichol Smith and Edward L. McAdam (Oxford, 1941), pp. 51–53.

Then crushed by rules, and weakened as refined,
For years the power of Tragedy declined;
From bard to bard, the frigid caution crept,
Till Declamation roared, while Passion slept.
Yet still did Virtue deign the stage to tread,
Philosophy remained, though Nature fled.
But forced at length her ancient reign to quit,
She saw great Faustus [1] lay the ghost of wit;
Exulting Folly hailed the joyful day,
And pantomime and song confirmed her sway.

But who the coming changes can presage
And mark the future periods of the stage?
Perhaps if skill could distant times explore,
New Behns,[2] new Durfeys [3] yet remain in store.
Perhaps where Lear has raved and Hamlet died,
On flying cars new sorcerers may ride.
Perhaps, for who can guess the effects of chance?
Here Hunt [4] may box, or Mahomet [5] may dance.

Hard is his lot that here by Fortune placed
Must watch the wild vicissitudes of taste,
With every meteor of caprice must play,
And chase the new-blown bubbles of the day.
Ah! let not Censure term our fate our choice;
The stage but echoes back the public voice.
The drama's laws the drama's patrons give,
For we that live to please must please to live.

Then prompt no more the follies you decry,
As tyrants doom their tools of guilt to die;

[1] "Harlequin Doctor Faustus" was the hero of a set of farci-
cal after-pieces which became the vogue both at Drury Lane
and Lincoln's Inn Fields during the 1720's. See Pope's *Dunciad
Variorum*, 1729, III, 229, 306.

[2] Afra Behn (1640–1689) was the author of a number of
coarse comedies concerning contemporary London life.

[3] Tom Durfey (1653–1723), poet and dramatist, was a
favorite butt of the wits during the time of Dryden and Pope.

[4] Edward Hunt was a contemporary lightweight boxer
"famous . . . on the stage."

[5] Mahomet was "a rope-dancer, who had exhibited at Covent
Garden Theatre the winter before, said to be a Turk" (*Works
of Johnson*, ed. Sir. John Hawkins, 1787, XI, 345).

'Tis yours this night to bid the reign commence
Of rescued Nature and reviving Sense;
To chase the charms of sound, the pomp of show,
For useful mirth and salutary woe;
Bid scenic Virtue form the rising age
And Truth diffuse her radiance from the stage.

TWO ESSAYS FROM *THE RAMBLER*[1] [1751]

Number 156. Saturday, September 14, 1751

Nunquam aliud natura, aliud sapientia dicit.
For Wisdom ever echoes Nature's voice.[2]

Juvenal [XIV. 321]

Every government, say the politicians, is perpetually degenerating towards corruption, from which it must be rescued at certain periods by the resuscitation of its first principles and the re-establishment of its original constitution. Every animal body, according to the methodic physicians, is, by the predominance of some exuberant quality, continually declining towards disease and death, which must be obviated by a seasonable reduction of the peccant humor to the just equipoise which health requires.

In the same manner the studies of mankind, all at least which, not being subject to rigorous demonstration, admit the influence of fancy and caprice, are perpetually tending to error and confusion. Of the great principles of truth which the first speculatists discovered, the simplicity is embarrassed by ambitious additions, or the evidence obscured by inaccurate argumentation; and as they descend from one succession of writers to another, like light transmitted from room to room, they lose their strength and splendor and fade at last in total evanescence.

The systems of learning therefore must be sometimes reviewed, complications analyzed into principles, and knowledge disentangled from opinion. It is not always

[1] The folio *Rambler* text of 1750–1752 was lightly revised by Johnson for a collected edition, six volumes in duodecimo, 1752, and again, more heavily, for the "Fourth" edition, four volumes in duodecimo, 1756. Johnson's revisions in the two *Ramblers* here presented were made chiefly, if not entirely, for the sake of simplifying his phrases and improving the diction. Our text follows the "Fourth" edition, without noticing any variations. The copy used is in the collection of Herman W. Liebert. The collation with the earlier texts was made by Albrecht B. Strauss. Walter Jackson Bate contributed to the annotations.

[2] The translation is by Johnson.

possible, without a close inspection, to separate the genuine shoots of consequential reasoning, which grow out of some radical postulate, from the branches which art has grafted on it. The accidental prescriptions of authority, when time has procured them veneration, are often confounded with the laws of nature, and those rules are supposed coeval with reason, of which the first rise cannot be discovered.

Criticism has sometimes permitted fancy to dictate the laws by which fancy ought to be restrained, and fallacy to perplex the principles by which fallacy is to be detected; her superintendence of others has betrayed her to negligence of herself; and, like the ancient Scythians, by extending her conquests over distant regions, she has left her throne vacant to her slaves.[1]

Among the laws of which the desire of extending authority or ardor of promoting knowledge has prompted the prescription, all which writers have received had not the same original right to our regard. Some are to be considered as fundamental and indispensable, others only as useful and convenient; some as dictated by reason and necessity, others as enacted by despotic antiquity; some as invincibly supported by their conformity to the order of nature and operations of the intellect, others as formed by accident or instituted by example and therefore always liable to dispute and alteration.

That many rules have been advanced without consulting nature or reason, we cannot but suspect when we find it peremptorily decreed by the ancient masters that *only three speaking personages should appear at once upon the stage;* [2] a law which, as the variety and intricacy of modern plays has made it impossible to be observed, we now violate without scruple and, as experience proves, without inconvenience.

The original of this precept was merely accidental. Tragedy was a monody or solitary song in honor of Bacchus, improved afterwards into a dialogue by the addition of another speaker; but the ancients, remembering that the tragedy was at first pronounced only by one, durst not for some time venture beyond two; at

[1] See Herodotus, IV. 1–4.
[2] See Aristotle, *Poetics,* Chapter IV; Horace, *Ars Poetica,* 1. 192: "nec quarta loqui persona laboret."

last, when custom and impunity had made them daring, they extended their liberty to the admission of three, but restrained themselves by a critical edict from further exorbitance.

By what accident the number of acts was limited to five, I know not that any author has informed us; but certainly it is not determined by any necessity arising either from the nature of action or propriety of exhibition. An act is only the representation of such a part of the business of the play as proceeds in an unbroken tenor or without any intermediate pause. Nothing is more evident than that of every real, and by consequence of every dramatic action, the intervals may be more or fewer than five; and indeed the rule is upon the English stage every day broken in effect, without any other mischief than that which arises from an absurd endeavor to observe it in appearance. Whenever the scene is shifted, the act ceases, since some time is necessarily supposed to elapse while the personages of the drama change their place.

With no greater right to our obedience have the critics confined the dramatic action to a certain number of hours. Probability requires that the time of action should approach somewhat nearly to that of exhibition, and those plays will always be thought most happily conducted which crowd the greatest variety into the least space. But since it will frequently happen that some delusion must be admitted, I know not where the limits of imagination can be fixed. It is rarely observed that minds not prepossessed by mechanical criticism feel any offense from the extension of the intervals between the acts; nor can I conceive it absurd or impossible that he who can multiply three hours into twelve or twenty-four might image with equal ease a greater number.

I know not whether he that professes to regard no other laws than those of nature will not be inclined to receive tragicomedy to his protection, whom, however generally condemned, her own laurels have hitherto shaded from the fulminations of criticism. For what is there in the mingled drama which impartial reason can condemn? The connection of important with trivial incidents, since it is not only common but perpetual in the world, may surely be allowed upon the stage, which pretends only to be the mirror of life. The impropriety of suppressing passions before we have raised them to the intended agitation, and of diverting the expectation from an event which we keep suspended only to raise it, may be speciously urged. But will not experience show this objection to be rather subtle than just? Is it not certain that the tragic and comic affections have been moved alternately with equal force, and that no plays have oftener filled the eye with tears and the breast with palpitation than those which are variegated with interludes of mirth? [1]

I do not, however, think it safe to judge of works of genius merely by the event. These resistless vicissitudes of the heart, this alternate prevalence of merriment and solemnity, may sometimes be more properly ascribed to the vigor of the writer than the justness of the design; and instead of vindicating tragicomedy by the success of Shakespeare, we ought perhaps to pay new honors to that transcendent and unbounded genius that could preside over the passions in sport; who, to actuate the affections, needed not the slow gradation of common means, but could fill the heart with instantaneous jollity or sorrow and vary our disposition as he changed his scenes. Perhaps the effects even of Shakespeare's poetry might have been yet greater had he not counteracted himself; and we might have been more interested in the distresses of his heroes had we not been so frequently diverted by the jokes of his buffoons.

There are other rules more fixed and obligatory. It is necessary that of every play the chief action should be single; for since a play represents some transaction, through its regular maturation to its final event, two actions equally important must evidently constitute two plays.

As the design of tragedy is to instruct by moving the passions, it must always have a hero, a personage apparently and incontestably superior to the rest, upon whom the attention may be fixed, and the anxiety suspended. For though of two persons opposing each other with equal abilities and equal virtue, the auditor

---

[1] The discussion of place and time on the stage, and of "mingled drama" in the preceding three paragraphs anticipates the *Preface* of 1765. See below, pp. 36–41.

will inevitably in time choose his favorite, yet as that choice must be without any cogency of conviction, the hopes or fears which it raises will be faint and languid. Of two heroes acting in confederacy against a common enemy, the virtues or dangers will give little emotion, because each claims our concern with the same right, and the heart lies at rest between equal motives.

It ought to be the first endeavor of a writer to distinguish nature from custom; or that which is established because it is right from that which is right only because it is established; that he may neither violate essential principles by a desire of novelty, nor debar himself from the attainment of beauties within his view, by a needless fear of breaking rules which no literary dictator had authority to enact.

Number 168. Saturday, October 26, 1751

Decipit
Frons prima multos, rara mens intelligit
Quod interiore condidit cura angulo.

Phaedrus [IV. ii. 5–7]

The tinsel glitter and the specious mien
Delude the most; few pry behind the scene.[1]

It has been observed by Boileau that "a mean or common thought expressed in pompous diction generally pleases more than a new or noble sentiment delivered in low and vulgar language; because the number is greater of those whom custom has enabled to judge of words than whom study has qualified to examine things."

This solution might satisfy if such only were offended with meanness of expression as are unable to distinguish propriety of thought and to separate propositions or images from the vehicles by which they are conveyed to the understanding. But this kind of disgust is by no means confined to the ignorant or superficial; it operates uniformly and universally upon readers of all classes; every man, however profound or abstracted, perceives

---

[1] The translation is by Johnson.

himself irresistibly alienated by low terms; they who profess the most zealous adherence to truth are forced to admit that she owes part of her charms to her ornaments and loses much of her power over the soul when she appears disgraced by a dress uncouth or ill-adjusted.

We are all offended by low terms but are not disgusted alike by the same compositions, because we do not all agree to censure the same terms as low. No word is naturally or intrinsically meaner than another; our opinion therefore of words, as of other things arbitrarily and capriciously established, depends wholly upon accident and custom. The cottager thinks those apartments splendid and spacious which an inhabitant of palaces will despise for their inelegance; and to him who has passed most of his hours with the delicate and polite, many expressions will seem sordid which another, equally acute, may hear without offense; but a mean term never fails to displease him to whom it appears mean, as poverty is certainly and invariably despised, though he who is poor in the eyes of some may by others be envied for his wealth.

Words become low by the occasions to which they are applied or the general character of them who use them; and the disgust which they produce arises from the revival of those images with which they are commonly united. Thus if, in the most solemn discourse, a phrase happens to occur which has been successfully employed in some ludicrous narrative, the gravest auditor finds it difficult to refrain from laughter, when they who are not prepossessed by the same accidental association are utterly unable to guess the reason of his merriment. Words which convey ideas of dignity in one age are banished from elegant writing or conversation in another, because they are in time debased by vulgar mouths and can be no longer heard without the involuntary recollection of unpleasing images.

When Macbeth is confirming himself in the horrid purpose of stabbing his king, he breaks out amidst his emotions into a wish natural to a murderer.

> Come, thick night,
> And pall thee in the dunnest smoke of hell,
> That my keen knife see not the wound it makes,

> Nor heaven peep through the blanket of the dark,
> To cry, 'Hold, hold!' [1]

In this passage is exerted all the force of poetry, that force which calls new powers into being, which embodies sentiment and animates matter; yet perhaps scarce any man now peruses it without some disturbance of his attention from the counteraction of the words to the ideas. What can be more dreadful than to implore the presence of the night, invested not in common obscurity, but in the smoke of hell? Yet the efficacy of this invocation is destroyed by the insertion of an epithet now seldom heard but in the stable, and *dun* night may come or go without any other notice than contempt.

If we start into raptures when some hero of the *Iliad* tells us that δόρυ μαίνεται,[2] his lance rages with eagerness to destroy; if we are alarmed at the terror of the soldiers commanded by Caesar to hew down the sacred grove, who dreaded, says Lucan, lest the axe aimed at the oak should fly back upon the striker—

> Si robora sacra ferirent,
> In sua credebant redituras membra secures,[3]
> None dares with impious steel the grove to rend,
> Lest on himself the destined stroke descend—

we cannot surely but sympathize with the horrors of a wretch about to murder his master, his friend, his benefactor, who suspects that the weapon will refuse its office and start back from the breast which he is preparing to violate. Yet this sentiment is weakened by the name of an instrument used by butchers and cooks in the meanest employments; we do not immediately conceive that any crime of importance is to be committed with a *knife;* or who does not, at last, from the long habit of connecting a knife with sordid offices, feel aversion rather than terror?

Macbeth proceeds to wish, in the madness of guilt, that the inspection of heaven may be intercepted, and that he may, in the involutions of infernal darkness, escape the eye of providence. This is the utmost extrava-

---

[1] *Macbeth,* I. v. 51–55. The words are spoken by Lady Macbeth.

[2] *Iliad,* VIII. 111.

[3] Lucan, *Pharsalia,* III. 430–431. The translation is by Johnson.

gance of determined wickedness; yet this is so debased
by two unfortunate words that while I endeavor to
impress on my reader the energy of the sentiment, I
can scarce check my risibility when the expression forces
itself upon my mind; for who, without some relaxation
of his gravity, can hear of the avengers of guilt *peeping
through a blanket?*

These imperfections of diction are less obvious to the
reader as he is less acquainted with common usages;
they are therefore wholly imperceptible to a foreigner,
who learns our language from books, and will strike a
solitary academic less forcibly than a modish lady.

Among the numerous requisites that most concur to
complete an author, few are of more importance than
an early entrance into the living world. The seeds of
knowledge may be planted in solitude but must be
cultivated in public. Argumentation may be taught in
colleges, and theories formed in retirement, but the artifice
of embellishment and the powers of attraction can be
gained only by general converse.

An acquaintance with prevailing customs and fashionable elegance is necessary likewise for other purposes.
The injury that grand imagery suffers from unsuitable
language, personal merit may fear from rudeness and
indelicacy. When the success of Aeneas depended on the
favor of the queen upon whose coasts he was driven,
his celestial protectress thought him not sufficiently
secured against rejection by his piety, or bravery, but
decorated him for the interview with preternatural
beauty.[1] Whoever desires, for his writings or himself, what
none can reasonably contemn, the favor of mankind, must
add grace to strength and make his thoughts agreeable
as well as useful. Many complain of neglect who never
tried to attract regard. It cannot be expected that the
patrons of science or virtue should be solicitous to discover
excellencies which they who possess them shade and disguise. Few have abilities so much needed by the rest of
the world as to be caressed on their own terms; and he
that will not condescend to recommend himself by external embellishments must submit to the fate of just sentiments meanly expressed and be ridiculed and forgotten
before he is understood.

[1] *Aeneid*, I. 586–593.

DEDICATION TO *SHAKESPEARE ILLUS-TRATED*[1] [1753]

To the Right Honorable John
Earl of Orrery

My Lord,

I have no other pretence to the honor of a patronage so illustrious as that of Your Lordship than the merit of attempting what has by some unaccountable neglect been hitherto omitted, though absolutely necessary to a perfect knowledge of the abilities of Shakespeare.

Among the powers that must conduce to constitute a poet, the first and most valuable is invention; and of all the degrees of invention, the highest seems to be that which is able to produce a series of events. It is easy when the thread of a story is once drawn to diversify it with variety of colors; and when a train of action is presented to the mind, a little acquaintance with life will supply circumstances and reflections, and a little knowledge of books, furnish parallels and illustrations. To tell over again a story that has been told already and to tell it better than the first author is no rare qualification; but to strike out the first hints of a new fable; hence to introduce a set of characters so diversified in their several passions and interests that from the clashing of this variety may result many necessary incidents; to make these incidents surprising and yet natural, so as to delight the imagination

[1] Written by Johnson for Mrs. Charlotte Ramsay Lennox. (See above, pp. xviii.) The text follows that of her *Shakespeare Illustrated,* two volumes, London, 1753. See also Allen T. Hazen, *Samuel Johnson's Prefaces & Dedications* (New Haven, 1937), pp. 108–110. John Boyle, 5th Earl of Orrery (1707–1762) had been a friend of Swift's and had recently published a *Life of Swift* and a translation of the younger Pliny's *Epistles.* He aspired to a literary eminence for which in Johnson's opinion he lacked the necessary force of mind and character. Johnson had introduced Mrs. Lennox to Orrery a few years earlier, and later Orrery was to help her with her translation of *The Greek Theater of Fr. Brumoy.* (See Miriam R. Small, *Charlotte Ramsay Lennox,* New Haven, 1935, pp. 12, 26.)

without shocking the judgment of a reader; and finally, to wind up the whole in a pleasing catastrophe produced by those very means which seem most likely to oppose and prevent it, is the utmost effort of the human mind.

To discover how few of those writers who profess to recount imaginary adventures have been able to produce any thing by their own imagination would require too much of that time which Your Lordship employs in nobler studies. Of all the novels and romances that wit or idleness, vanity or indigence have pushed into the world, there are very few of which the end cannot be conjectured from the beginning, or where the authors have done more than to transpose the incidents of other tales or strip the circumstances from one event for the decoration of another.

In the examination of a poet's character it is therefore first to be inquired what degree of invention has been exerted by him. With this view I have very diligently read the works of Shakespeare and now presume to lay the result of my searches before Your Lordship, before that judge whom Pliny himself would have wished for his assessor to hear a literary cause.[1]

How much the translation of the following novels will add to the reputation of Shakespeare or take away from it, you, My Lord, and men learned and candid like you, if any such can be found, must now determine. Some danger, as I am informed, there is, lest his admirers should think him injured by this attempt and clamor as at the diminution of the honor of that nation which boasts herself the parent of so great a poet.

That no such enemies may arise against me (though I am unwilling to believe it) I am far from being too confident, for who can fix bounds to bigotry and folly? My sex, my age have not given me many opportunities of mingling in the world; there may be in it many a species of absurdity which I have never seen, and among them such vanity as pleases itself with false praise bestowed on another, and such superstition as worships idols without supposing them to be gods.

But the truth is that a very small part of the reputation

---

[1] Pliny the Elder in the Preface to his *Natural History* dedicates the work to the Emperor Titus with fulsome flattery of his powers as a critic and judge.

of this mighty genius depends upon the naked plot or story of his plays. He lived in an age when the books of chivalry were yet popular, and when therefore the minds of his auditors were not accustomed to balance probabilities or to examine nicely the proportion between causes and effects. It was sufficient to recommend a story, that it was far removed from common life, that its changes were frequent and its close pathetic.

This disposition of the age concurred so happily with the imagination of Shakespeare that he had no desire to reform it, and indeed to this he was indebted for the licentious variety by which he has made his plays more entertaining then those of any other author.

He had looked with great attention on the scenes of nature; but his chief skill was in human actions, passions, and habits; he was therefore delighted with such tales as afforded numerous incidents and exhibited many characters in many changes of situation. These characters are so copiously diversified, and some of them so justly pursued, that his works may be considered as a map of life, a faithful miniature of human transactions, and he that has read Shakespeare with attention will perhaps find little new in the crowded world.

Among his other excellencies it ought to be remarked, because it has hitherto been unnoticed, that his heroes are men, that the love and hatred, and hopes and fears of his chief personages are such as are common to other human beings, and not like those which later times have exhibited, peculiar to phantoms that strut upon the stage.

It is not perhaps very necessary to inquire whether the vehicle of so much delight and instruction be a story probable, or unlikely, native, or foreign. Shakespeare's excellence is not the fiction of a tale but the representation of life; and his reputation is therefore safe till human nature shall be changed. Nor can he who has so many just claims to praise suffer by losing that which ignorant admiration has unreasonably given him. To calumniate the dead is baseness, and to flatter them is surely folly.

From flattery, My Lord, either of the dead or the living, I wish to be clear and have therefore solicited the countenance of a patron whom, if I knew how to praise him, I would praise with truth and have the world on my side; whose candor and humanity are universally acknowl-

edged, and whose judgment perhaps was then first to be
doubted when he condescended to admit this address
from,

   My Lord, Your Lordship's most obliged and most
obedient, humble servant,

The Author.

PROPOSALS [1756]

For Printing by Subscription
The Dramatic Works of William Shakespeare
Corrected and Illustrated
By Samuel Johnson [1]

When the works of Shakespeare are, after so many editions, again offered to the public, it will doubtless be inquired why Shakespeare stands in more need of critical assistance than any other of the English writers, and what are the deficiencies of the late attempts which another editor may hope to supply?

The business of him that republishes an ancient book is to correct what is corrupt and to explain what is obscure. To have a text corrupt in many places, and in many doubtful, is, among the authors that have written since the use of types, almost peculiar to Shakespeare. Most writers, by publishing their own works, prevent all various readings and preclude all conjectural criticism. Books indeed are sometimes published after the death of him that produced them; but they are better secured from corruption than these unfortunate compositions. They subsist in a single copy, written or revised by the author; and the faults of the printed volume can be only faults of one descent.

But of the works of Shakespeare the condition has been far different. He sold them, not to be printed, but to be played. They were immediately copied for the actors and multiplied by transcript after transcript, vitiated by the blunders of the penman or changed by the affectation of the player; perhaps enlarged to introduce a jest or mutilated to shorten the representation; and printed at last without the concurrence of the author, without the consent of the proprietor, from compilations made by chance or by stealth out of the separate parts written for the theater; and thus thrust into the world surreptitiously and hastily, they suffered another depravation

[1] The text follows the first edition, *Proposals for Printing by Subscription the Dramatic Works of William Shakespeare, Corrected and Illustrated by Samuel Johnson,* London, 1756 (Facsimile, Oxford, 1923).

from the ignorance and negligence of the printers, as every man who knows the state of the press in that age will readily conceive.

It is not easy for invention to bring together so many causes concurring to vitiate a text. No other author ever gave up his works to fortune and time with so little care; no books could be left in hands so likely to injure them as plays frequently acted yet continued in manuscript; no other transcribers were likely to be so little qualified for their task as those who copied for the stage, at a time when the lower ranks of the people were universally illiterate; no other editions were made from fragments so minutely broken and so fortuitously reunited; and in no other age was the art of printing in such unskillful hands.

With the causes of corruption that make the revisal of Shakespeare's dramatic pieces necessary, may be enumerated the causes of obscurity, which may be partly imputed to his age and partly to himself.

When a writer outlives his contemporaries and remains almost the only unforgotten name of a distant time, he is necessarily obscure. Every age has its modes of speech and its cast of thought; which, though easily explained when there are many books to be compared with each other, become sometimes unintelligible and always difficult when there are no parallel passages that may conduce to their illustration. Shakespeare is the first considerable author of sublime or familiar dialogue in our language. Of the books which he read, and from which he formed his style, some perhaps have perished, and the rest are neglected. His imitations are therefore unnoted, his allusions are undiscovered, and many beauties, both of pleasantry and greatness, are lost with the objects to which they were united, as the figures vanish when the canvas has decayed.

It is the great excellence of Shakespeare that he drew his scenes from nature and from life. He copied the manners of the world then passing before him and has more allusions than other poets to the traditions and superstition of the vulgar; which must therefore be traced before he can be understood.

He wrote at a time when our poetical language was yet unformed, when the meaning of our phrases was yet in fluctuation, when words were adopted at pleasure from the neighboring languages, and while the Saxon was still visibly mingled in our diction. The reader is therefore embarrassed at once with dead and foreign languages, with obsoleteness and innovation. In that age, as in all others, fashion produced phraseology which succeeding fashion swept away before its meaning was generally known or sufficiently authorized; and in that age, above all others, experiments were made upon our language which distorted its combinations and disturbed its uniformity.

If Shakespeare has difficulties above other writers, it is to be imputed to the nature of his work, which required the use of the common colloquial language and consequently admitted many phrases allusive, elliptical, and proverbial, such as we speak and hear every hour without observing them; and of which, being now familiar, we do not suspect that they can ever grow uncouth, or that, being now obvious, they can ever seem remote.

These are the principal causes of the obscurity of Shakespeare; to which might be added that fullness of idea which might sometimes load his words with more sentiment than they could conveniently convey, and that rapidity of imagination which might hurry him to a second thought before he had fully explained the first. But my opinion is that very few of his lines were difficult to his audience, and that he used such expressions as were then common, though the paucity of contemporary writers makes them now seem peculiar.

Authors are often praised for improvement, or blamed for innovation, with very little justice, by those who read few other books of the same age. Addison himself has been so unsuccessful in enumerating the words with which Milton has enriched our language as perhaps not to have named one of which Milton was the author; and Bentley has yet more unhappily praised him as the introducer of those elisions into English poetry which had been used from the first essays of versification among us, and which Milton was indeed the last that practiced.

Another impediment, not the least vexatious to the commentator, is the exactness with which Shakespeare followed his authors. Instead of dilating his thoughts into generalities and expressing incidents with poetic latitude, he often combines circumstances unnecessary to his main design, only because he happened to find them together. Such passages can be illustrated only by him who has read the same story in the very book which Shakespeare consulted.

He that undertakes an edition of Shakespeare has all these difficulties to encounter and all these obstructions to remove.

The corruptions of the text will be corrected by a careful collation of the oldest copies, by which it is hoped that many restorations may yet be made; at least it will be necessary to collect and note the variations as materials for future critics; for it very often happens that a wrong reading has affinity to the right.

In this part all the present editions are apparently and intentionally defective. The critics did not so much as wish to facilitate the labor of those that followed them. The same books are still to be compared; the work that has been done is to be done again; and no single edition will supply the reader with a text on which he can rely as the best copy of the works of Shakespeare.

The edition now proposed will at least have this advantage over others. It will exhibit all the observable varieties of all the copies that can be found; that, if the reader is not satisfied with the editor's determination, he may have the means of choosing better for himself.

Where all the books are evidently vitiated, and collation can give no assistance, then begins the task of critical sagacity; and some changes may well be admitted in a text never settled by the author and so long exposed to caprice and ignorance. But nothing shall be imposed, as in the Oxford edition, without notice of the alteration; nor shall conjecture be wantonly or unnecessarily indulged.

It has been long found that very specious emendations do not equally strike all minds with conviction, nor even the same mind at different times; and therefore, though perhaps many alterations may be proposed as eligible, very few will be obtruded as certain. In a language so ungrammatical as the English and so licentious as that of Shakespeare, emendatory criticism is always hazardous; nor can it be allowed to any man who is not particularly versed in the writings of that age and particularly studious of his author's diction. There is danger lest peculiarities should be mistaken for corruptions, and passages rejected as unintelligible, which a narrow mind happens not to understand.

All the former critics have been so much employed on the correction of the text that they have not sufficiently attended to the elucidation of passages obscured by accident or time. The editor will endeavor to read the books which the author read, to trace his knowledge to its source and compare his copies with their originals. If in this part of his design he hopes to attain any degree of superiority to his predecessors, it must be considered that he has the advantage of their labors; that part of the work being already done, more care is naturally bestowed on the other part; and that, to declare the truth, Mr. Rowe and Mr. Pope were very ignorant of the ancient English literature; Dr. Warburton was detained by more important studies; and Mr. Theobald, if fame be just to his memory, considered learning only as an instrument of gain and made no further inquiry after his author's meaning when once he had notes sufficient to embellish his page with the expected decorations.

With regard to obsolete or peculiar diction, the editor may perhaps claim some degree of confidence, having had more motives to consider the whole extent of our language than any other man from its first formation. He hopes that, by comparing the works of Shakespeare with those of writers who lived at the same time, immediately preceded, or immediately followed him, he shall be able to ascertain his ambiguities, disentangle his intricacies, and recover the meaning of words now lost in the darkness of antiquity.

When therefore any obscurity arises from an allusion to some other book, the passage will be quoted. When the diction is entangled, it will be cleared by a paraphrase or interpretation. When the sense is broken by the suppression of part of the sentiment in pleasantry or passion, the connection will be supplied. When any forgotten custom is hinted, care will be taken to retrieve and explain it. The meaning assigned to doubtful words will be supported by the authorities of other writers or by parallel passages of Shakespeare himself.

The observation of faults and beauties is one of the duties of an annotator which some of Shakespeare's editors have attempted and some have neglected. For this part of his task, and for this only, was Mr. Pope eminently and indisputably qualified; nor has Dr. Warburton followed him with less diligence or less success. But I have never observed that mankind was much delighted or improved by their asterisks, commas, or double commas; of which the only effect is that they preclude the pleasure of judging for ourselves; teach the young and ignorant to decide without principles; defeat curiosity and discernment, by leaving them less to discover; and at last show the opinion of the critic without the reasons on which it was founded, and without affording any light by which it may be examined.

The editor, though he may less delight his own vanity, will probably please his reader more, by supposing him equally able with himself to judge of beauties and faults which require no previous acquisition of remote knowledge. A description of the obvious scenes of nature, a representation of general life, a sentiment of reflection or experience, a deduction of conclusive argument, a forcible eruption of effervescent passion, are to be considered as proportionate to common apprehension, unassisted by critical officiousness; since, to conceive them, nothing more is requisite than acquaintance with the general state of the world, and those faculties which he must always bring with him who would read Shakespeare.

But when the beauty arises from some adaptation of the sentiment to customs worn out of use, to opinions not universally prevalent, or to any accidental or minute particularity which cannot be supplied by common understanding or common observation, it is the duty of a commentator to lend his assistance.

The notice of beauties and faults thus limited will make no distinct part of the design, being reducible to the explanation of obscure passages.

The editor does not, however, intend to preclude himself from the comparison of Shakespeare's sentiments or expression with those of ancient or modern authors, or from the display of any beauty not obvious to the students of poetry; for as he hopes to leave his author better understood, he wishes likewise to procure him more rational approbation.

The former editors have affected to slight their predecessors; but in this edition all that is valuable will be
adopted from every commentator, that posterity may
consider it as including all the rest and exhibiting whatever
is hitherto known of the great father of the English
drama.

PREFACE [1765]

To Johnson's edition of
The Plays of William Shakespeare, 1765 [1]

That praises are without reason lavished on the dead, and that the honors due only to excellence are paid to antiquity, is a complaint likely to be always continued by those who, being able to add nothing to truth, hope for eminence from the heresies of paradox; or those who, being forced by disappointment upon consolatory expedients, are willing to hope from posterity what the present age refuses and flatter themselves that the regard which is yet denied by envy will be at last bestowed by time.

Antiquity, like every other quality that attracts the notice of mankind, has undoubtedly votaries that reverence it, not from reason, but from prejudice. Some seem to admire indiscriminately whatever has been long preserved, without considering that time has sometimes cooperated with chance; all perhaps are more willing to honor past than present excellence; and the mind contemplates genius through the shades of age, as the eye surveys the sun through artificial opacity. The great contention of criticism is to find the faults of the moderns and the beauties of the ancients. While an author is yet living, we estimate his powers by his worst performance; and when he is dead, we rate them by his best.

To works, however, of which the excellence is not absolute and definite, but gradual and comparative; to works not raised upon principles demonstrative and scientific, but appealing wholly to observation and experience, no other test can be applied than length of duration and continuance of esteem. What mankind have long possessed they have often examined and compared; and if they persist to value the possession, it is because frequent comparisons have confirmed opinion in its favor. As among the works of nature no man can properly call a river deep or a mountain high, without the knowl-

---

[1] The text follows the first printing of 1765. But a few more important changes made from 1773 to 1780 have been adopted and are duly indicated.

edge of many mountains and many rivers; so, in the productions of genius, nothing can be styled excellent till it has been compared with other works of the same kind. Demonstration immediately displays its power and has nothing to hope or fear from the flux of years; but works tentative and experimental must be estimated by their proportion to the general and collective ability of man, as it is discovered in a long succession of endeavors. Of the first building that was raised, it might be with certainty determined that it was round or square, but whether it was spacious or lofty must have been referred to time. The Pythagorean scale of numbers [1] was at once discovered to be perfect; but the poems of Homer we yet know not to transcend the common limits of human intelligence but by remarking that nation after nation, and century after century, has been able to do little more than transpose his incidents, new-name his characters, and paraphrase his sentiments.

The reverence due to writings that have long subsisted arises, therefore, not from any credulous confidence in the superior wisdom of past ages or gloomy persuasion of the degeneracy of mankind, but is the consequence of acknowledged and indubitable positions, that what has been longest known has been most considered, and what is most considered is best understood.

The poet of whose works I have undertaken the revision may now begin to assume the dignity of an ancient and claim the privilege of established fame and prescriptive veneration. He has long outlived his century, the term commonly fixed as the test of literary merit. Whatever advantages he might once derive from personal allusions, local customs, or temporary opinions have for many years been lost; and every topic of merriment or motive of sorrow which the modes of artificial life afforded him now only obscure the scenes which they once illuminated. The effects of favor and competition are at an end; the tradition of his friendships and his enmities have perished; his works support no opinion with arguments nor supply any faction with invectives; they can neither indulge vanity nor gratify malignity; but are read without any other reason than the desire of pleasure and are therefore praised only as pleasure is obtained; yet, thus

[1] See Aristotle, *Metaphysics*, I. 5.

unassisted by interest or passion, they have passed through variations of taste and changes of manners, and, as they devolved from one generation to another, have received new honors at every transmission.

But because human judgment, though it be gradually gaining upon certainty, never becomes infallible; and approbation, though long continued, may yet be only the approbation of prejudice or fashion; it is proper to inquire by what peculiarities of excellence Shakespeare has gained and kept the favor of his countrymen.

Nothing can please many, and please long, but just representations of general nature. Particular manners can be known to few, and therefore few only can judge how nearly they are copied. The irregular combinations of fanciful invention may delight awhile by that novelty of which the common satiety of life sends us all in quest; but the pleasures of sudden wonder are soon exhausted, and the mind can only repose on the stability of truth.

Shakespeare is, above all writers, at least above all modern writers, the poet of nature, the poet that holds up to his readers a faithful mirror of manners and of life. His characters are not modified by the customs of particular places, unpracticed by the rest of the world; by the peculiarities of studies or professions which can operate but upon small numbers; or by the accidents of transient fashions or temporary opinions: they are the genuine progeny of common humanity, such as the world will always supply, and observation will always find. His persons act and speak by the influence of those general passions and principles by which all minds are agitated and the whole system of life is continued in motion. In the writings of other poets a character is too often an individual; in those of Shakespeare it is commonly a species.

It is from this wide extension of design that so much instruction is derived. It is this which fills the plays of Shakespeare with practical axioms and domestic wisdom. It was said of Euripides that every verse was a precept; [1] and it may be said of Shakespeare that from his works may be collected a system of civil and economical prudence. Yet his real power is not shown in the splendor of particular passages, but by the progress of his fable and

[1] See Cicero, *Epistolae ad Familiares,* XVI. 8.

the tenor of his dialogue; and he that tries to recommend him by select quotations will succeed like the pedant in Hierocles, who, when he offered his house to sale, carried a brick in his pocket as a specimen.[1]

It will not easily be imagined how much Shakespeare excels in accommodating his sentiments to real life but by comparing him with other authors. It was observed of the ancient schools of declamation that the more diligently they were frequented, the more was the student disqualified for the world, because he found nothing there which he should ever meet in any other place.[2] The same remark may be applied to every stage but that of Shakespeare. The theater, when it is under any other direction, is peopled by such characters as were never seen, conversing in a language which was never heard, upon topics which will never arise in the commerce of mankind. But the dialogue of this author is often so evidently determined by the incident which produces it, and is pursued with so much ease and simplicity, that it seems scarcely to claim the merit of fiction, but to have been gleaned by diligent selection out of common conversation and common occurrences.

Upon every other stage the universal agent is love, by whose power all good and evil is distributed and every action quickened or retarded. To bring a lover, a lady, and a rival into the fable; to entangle them in contradictory obligations, perplex them with oppositions of interest, and harass them with violence of desires inconsistent with each other; to make them meet in rapture and part in agony, to fill their mouths with hyperbolical joy and outrageous sorrow, to distress them as nothing human ever was distressed, to deliver them as nothing human ever was delivered, is the business of a modern dramatist. For this, probability is violated, life is misrepresented, and language is depraved. But love is only one of many passions; and as it has no great influence upon the sum of life, it has little operation in the dramas of a poet who caught his ideas from the living world and

---

[1] Hierocles was a neo-Platonic Alexandrian of the fifth century A.D. The passage to which Johnson alludes appears in *Hieroclis Commentarius in Aurea Carmina,* ed. Needham, 1709, p. 462, *Asteia* No. 9 (attributed to Hierocles).

[2] See Petronius, *Satyricon,* I. 1.

exhibited only what he saw before him. He knew that any other passion, as it was regular or exorbitant, was a cause of happiness or calamity.

Characters thus ample and general were not easily discriminated and preserved, yet perhaps no poet ever kept his personages more distinct from each other. I will not say with Pope that every speech may be assigned to the proper speaker,[1] because many speeches there are which have nothing characteristical; but, perhaps, though some may be equally adapted to every person, it will be difficult to find any that can be properly transferred from the present possessor to another claimant. The choice is right, when there is reason for choice.

Other dramatists can only gain attention by hyperbolical or aggravated characters, by fabulous and unexampled excellence or depravity, as the writers of barbarous romances invigorated the reader by a giant and a dwarf; and he that should form his expectations of human affairs from the play, or from the tale, would be equally deceived. Shakespeare has no heroes; his scenes are occupied only by men, who act and speak as the reader thinks that he should himself have spoken or acted on the same occasion. Even where the agency is supernatural, the dialogue is level with life. Other writers disguise the most natural passions and most frequent incidents; so that he who contemplates them in the book will not know them in the world. Shakespeare approximates the remote and familiarizes the wonderful; the event which he represents will not happen, but, if it were possible, its effects would probably be such as he has assigned; and it may be said that he has not only shown human nature as it acts in real exigences, but as it would be found in trials to which it cannot be exposed.

This, therefore, is the praise of Shakespeare, that his drama is the mirror of life; that he who has mazed his imagination in following the phantoms which other writers raise up before him, may here be cured of his delirious ecstasies by reading human sentiments in human language, by scenes from which a hermit may estimate the transactions of the world and a confessor predict the progress of the passions.

His adherence to general nature has exposed him to

[1] Pope's *Preface* (1725), ¶ 4.

the censure of critics who form their judgments upon
narrower principles. Dennis and Rymer think his Romans
not sufficiently Roman; [1] and Voltaire censures his kings
as not completely royal. Dennis is offended that Menenius,
a senator of Rome, should play the buffoon; [2] and Voltaire perhaps thinks decency violated when the Danish
usurper is represented as a drunkard.[3] But Shakespeare
always makes nature predominate over accident; and, if
he preserves the essential character, is not very careful
of distinctions superinduced and adventitious. His story
requires Romans or kings, but he thinks only on men.
He knew that Rome, like every other city, had men of
all dispositions; and wanting a buffoon, he went into the
senate house for that which the senate house would certainly have afforded him. He was inclined to show an
usurper and a murderer not only odious, but despicable;
he therefore added drunkenness to his other qualities,
knowing that kings love wine like other men, and that
wine exerts its natural power upon kings. These are the
petty cavils of petty minds; a poet overlooks the casual
distinction of country and condition, as a painter, satisfied
with the figure, neglects the drapery.

The censure which he has incurred by mixing comic and
tragic scenes, as it extends to all his works, deserves
more consideration. Let the fact be first stated and then
examined.

Shakespeare's plays are not in the rigorous and critical

[1] See John Dennis, *An Essay on the Genius and Writings of
Shakespeare*, 1712; Thomas Rymer, *A Short View of Tragedy:
Its Original Excellency and Corruption, with Some Reflections
on Shakespeare and Other Practitioners for the Stage*, 1693.
The *Critical Works* of John Dennis have been edited by E. N.
Hooker, 2 vols. Baltimore, 1939–1943 (for the present reference
see II, 5–6); and the *Critical Works* of Rymer, by Curt A.
Zimansky, New Haven, 1956 (see pp. 164–169).

[2] *Essay on the Genius and Writings of Shakespeare*, in *Critical Works*, ed. Hooker, II, 5.

[3] Voltaire pronounces a general censure on the conversation of Shakespeare's "princes" in *L'Appel à toutes les nations
d'Europe*, 1761 (*Oeuvres*, ed. Moland, XXIV, 203). In his
Dissertation sur la tragédie ancienne et moderne, 1749, he
notices a number of *grossièretés* in *Hamlet*. Such a work seems
to him "the fruit of the imagination of a drunken savage"
(*Oeuvres*, ed. Moland, IV, 502). The word "perhaps" in Johnson's phrase about the Danish drunkard may indicate a degree
of extrapolation.

sense either tragedies or comedies, but compositions of a
distinct kind; exhibiting the real state of sublunary nature,
which partakes of good and evil, joy and sorrow, mingled
with endless variety of proportion and innumerable modes
of combination; and expressing the course of the world,
in which the loss of one is the gain of another; in which,
at the same time, the reveller is hasting to his wine, and
the mourner burying his friend; in which the malignity
of one is sometimes defeated by the frolic of another;
and many mischiefs and many benefits are done and
hindered without design.

Out of this chaos of mingled purposes and casualties
the ancient poets, according to the laws which custom
had prescribed, selected some the crimes of men, and some
their absurdities; some the momentous vicissitudes of life,
and some the lighter occurrences; some the terrors of
distress, and some the gaieties of prosperity. Thus rose the
two modes of imitation, known by the names of *tragedy*
and *comedy*, compositions intended to promote different
ends by contrary means, and considered as so little allied
that I do not recollect among the Greeks or Romans a
single writer who attempted both.

Shakespeare has united the powers of exciting laughter
and sorrow not only in one mind but in one composition.
Almost all his plays are divided between serious and ludicrous characters, and, in the successive evolutions of the
design, sometimes produce seriousness and sorrow, and
sometimes levity and laughter.

That this is a practice contrary to the rules of criticism will be readily allowed; but there is always an appeal
open from criticism to nature. The end of writing is to
instruct; the end of poetry is to instruct by pleasing.
That the mingled drama may convey all the instruction
of tragedy or comedy cannot be denied, because it includes
both in its alternations [1] of exhibition and approaches
nearer than either to the appearance of life, by showing how great machinations and slender designs may promote or obviate one another, and the high and the low
co-operate in the general system by unavoidable con-
catenation.

It is objected that by this change of scenes the passions

[1] 1765, 1768, 1773, 1778 read "alterations." The change was
made in 1780.

are interrupted in their progression, and that the principal
event, being not advanced by a due gradation of pre-
paratory incidents, wants at last the power to move,
which constitutes the perfection of dramatic poetry.
This reasoning is so specious that it is received as true
even by those who in daily experience feel it to be false.
The interchanges of mingled scenes seldom fail to produce
the intended vicissitudes of passion. Fiction cannot move
so much but that the attention may be easily transferred;
and though it must be allowed that pleasing melancholy
be sometimes interrupted by unwelcome levity, yet let
it be considered likewise that melancholy is often not
pleasing, and that the disturbance of one man may be
the relief of another; that different auditors have different
habitudes; and that, upon the whole, all pleasure consists
in variety.

The players, who in their edition [1] divided our author's
works into comedies, histories, and tragedies, seem not
to have distinguished the three kinds by any very exact
or definite ideas.

An action which ended happily to the principal persons,
however serious or distressful through its intermediate
incidents, in their opinion constituted a comedy. This
idea of a comedy continued long amongst us; and plays
were written which, by changing the catastrophe, were
tragedies today and comedies tomorrow.

Tragedy was not in those times a poem of more
general dignity or elevation than comedy; it required only
a calamitous conclusion, with which the common criticism
of the age was satisfied, whatever lighter pleasure it
afforded in its progress.

History was a series of actions, with no other than
chronological succession, independent on [2] each other,
and without any tendency to introduce or regulate the
conclusion. It is not always very nicely distinguished from
tragedy. There is not much nearer approach to unity of
action in the tragedy of *Antony and Cleopatra* than in
the history of *Richard the Second*. But a history might be

---

[1] John Heming and Henry Condell, friends of Shakespeare
and fellow actors, issued the First Folio in 1623.

[2] 1765 first printing has "on," changed to "of" in 1765 second
printing and back to "on" in 1773.

continued through many plays; as it had no plan, it had
no limits.

Through all these denominations of the drama,
Shakespeare's mode of composition is the same: an interchange of seriousness and merriment, by which the mind
is softened at one time and exhilarated at another. But
whatever be his purpose, whether to gladden or depress,
or to conduct the story, without vehemence or emotion,
through tracts of easy and familiar dialogue, he never fails
to attain his purpose; as he commands us, we laugh or
mourn, or sit silent with quiet expectation, in tranquillity
without indifference.

When Shakespeare's plan is understood, most of the
criticisms of Rymer and Voltaire vanish away. The play
of *Hamlet* is opened, without impropriety, by two sen-
tinels; Iago bellows at Brabantio's window without injury
to the scheme of the play, though in terms which a
modern audience would not easily endure; the character
of Polonius is seasonable and useful; and the gravediggers
themselves may be heard with applause.[1]

Shakespeare engaged in dramatic poetry with the world
open before him; the rules of the ancients were yet known
to few; the public judgment was unformed; he had no
example of such fame as might force him upon imitation,
nor critics of such authority as might restrain his extrava-
gance; he therefore indulged his natural disposition; and
his disposition, as Rymer has remarked, led him to
comedy.[2] In tragedy he often writes, with great appearance
of toil and study, what is written at last with little felicity;
but, in his comic scenes, he seems to produce, without
labor, what no labor can improve. In tragedy he is always struggling after some occasion to be comic; but
in comedy he seems to repose, or to luxuriate, as in a
mode of thinking congenial to his nature. In his tragic
scenes there is always something wanting, but his comedy
often surpasses expectation or desire. His comedy pleases
by the thoughts and the language, and his tragedy for

---

[1] The censures of *Hamlet* and *Othello* which Johnson answers
in this paragraph are to be found in Voltaire, *L'Appel* (*Oeuvres*,
ed. Moland, XXIV, 193, 196, 198, 204, 208) and in Rymer, *A
Short View of Tragedy* (*Works*, ed. Zimansky, pp. 131–164).
[2] *A Short View of Tragedy* (*Works*, ed. Zimansky, p. 169).

the greater part by incident and action. His tragedy
seems to be skill, his comedy to be instinct.

The force of his comic scenes has suffered little diminution, from the changes made by a century and a half,
in manners or in words. As his personages act upon
principles arising from genuine passion, very little modified
by particular forms, their pleasures and vexations are
communicable to all times and to all places; they are
natural, and therefore durable. The adventitious peculiarities of personal habits are only superficial dyes, bright
and pleasing for a little while, yet soon fading to a dim
tinct, without any remains of former lustre; but the discriminations of true passion are the colors of nature;
they pervade the whole mass and can only perish with
the body that exhibits them. The accidental compositions
of heterogeneous modes are dissolved by the chance which
combined them; but the uniform simplicity of primitive
qualities neither admits increase nor suffers decay. The
sand heaped by one flood is scattered by another, but the
rock always continues in its place. The stream of time,
which is continually washing the dissoluble fabrics of other
poets, passes without injury by the adamant of Shakespeare.

If there be, what I believe there is, in every nation
a style which never becomes obsolete, a certain mode of
phraseology so consonant and congenial to the analogy
and principles of its respective language as to remain
settled and unaltered; this style is probably to be sought
in the common intercourse of life, among those who
speak only to be understood, without ambition of elegance. The polite are always catching modish innova-
tions, and the learned depart from established forms of
speech in hope of finding or making better; those who
wish for distinction forsake the vulgar, when the vulgar
is right; but there is a conversation above grossness
and below refinement, where propriety resides, and where
this poet seems to have gathered his comic dialogue.
He is therefore more agreeable to the ears of the present
age than any other author equally remote and among
his other excellencies deserves to be studied as one of the
original masters of our language.

These observations are to be considered not as unexcep-
tionably constant, but as containing general and pre-

dominant truth. Shakespeare's familiar dialogue is affirmed to be smooth and clear, yet not wholly without ruggedness or difficulty; as a country may be eminently fruitful, though it has spots unfit for cultivation; his characters are praised as natural, though their sentiments are sometimes forced and their actions improbable; as the earth upon the whole is spherical, though its surface is varied with protuberances and cavities.

Shakespeare with his excellencies has likewise faults, and faults sufficient to obscure and overwhelm any other merit. I shall show them in the proportion in which they appear to me, without envious malignity or superstitious veneration. No question can be more innocently discussed than a dead poet's pretensions to renown; and little regard is due to that bigotry which sets candor higher than truth.

His first defect is that to which may be imputed most of the evil in books or in men. He sacrifices virtue to convenience and is so much more careful to please than to instruct that he seems to write without any moral purpose. From his writings indeed a system of social duty may be selected, for he that thinks reasonably must think morally; but his precepts and axioms drop casually from him; he makes no just distribution of good or evil, nor is always careful to show in the virtuous a disapprobation of the wicked; he carries his persons indifferently through right and wrong and at the close dismisses them without further care and leaves their examples to operate by chance. This fault the barbarity of his age cannot extenuate; for it is always a writer's duty to make the world better, and justice is a virtue independent on time or place.

The plots are often so loosely formed that a very slight consideration may improve them, and so carelessly pursued that he seems not always fully to comprehend his own design. He omits opportunities of instructing or delighting which the train of his story seems to force upon him, and apparently rejects those exhibitions which would be more affecting, for the sake of those which are more easy.

It may be observed that in many of his plays the latter part is evidently neglected. When he found himself near the end of his work, and in view of his reward, he shortened the labor to snatch the profit. He therefore remits his

efforts where he should most vigorously exert them, and
his catastrophe is improbably produced or imperfectly represented.

He had no regard to distinction of time or place, but
gives to one age or nation, without scruple, the customs,
institutions, and opinions of another, at the expense not
only of likelihood but of possibility. These faults Pope has
endeavored, with more zeal than judgment, to transfer to
his imagined interpolators.[1] We need not wonder to find
Hector quoting Aristotle,[2] when we see the loves of Theseus
and Hippolyta combined with the Gothic mythology of
fairies.[3] Shakespeare, indeed, was not the only violator of
chronology, for in the same age Sidney, who wanted not
the advantages of learning, has, in his *Arcadia*, confounded
the pastoral with the feudal times, the days of innocence,
quiet, and security, with those of turbulence, violence, and
adventure.

In his comic scenes he is seldom very successful when
he engages his characters in reciprocations of smartness
and contests of sarcasm; their jests are commonly gross,
and their pleasantry licentious; neither his gentlemen nor
his ladies have much delicacy nor are sufficiently distinguished from his clowns by any appearance of refined
manners. Whether he represented the real conversation of
his time is not easy to determine. The reign of Elizabeth
is commonly supposed to have been a time of stateliness,
formality, and reserve; yet perhaps the relaxations of that
severity were not very elegant. There must, however, have
been always some modes of gaiety preferable to others,
and a writer ought to choose the best.

In tragedy his performance seems constantly to be worse
as his labor is more. The effusions of passion which exi-
gence forces out are for the most part striking and energetic; but whenever he solicits his invention, or strains his
faculties, the offspring of his throes is tumor, meanness,
tediousness, and obscurity.

In narration he affects a disproportionate pomp of diction and a wearisome train of circumlocution and tells the
incident imperfectly in many words which might have
been more plainly delivered in few. Narration in dramatic
poetry is naturally tedious, as it is unanimated and inac-

1 Pope's *Preface to Shakespeare,* ¶ 22 ff.
2 *Troilus and Cressida,* II. ii. 166–167.
3 *A Midsummer Night's Dream,* throughout.

tive and obstructs the progress of the action; it should therefore always be rapid and enlivened by frequent interruption. Shakespeare found it an incumbrance and, instead of lightening it by brevity, endeavored to recommend it by dignity and splendor.

His declamations or set speeches are commonly cold and weak, for his power was the power of nature; when he endeavored, like other tragic writers, to catch opportunities of amplification, and, instead of inquiring what the occasion demanded, to show how much his stores of knowledge could supply, he seldom escapes without the pity or resentment of his reader.

It is incident to him to be now and then entangled with an unwieldy sentiment, which he cannot well express and will not reject; he struggles with it awhile, and, if it continues stubborn, comprises it in words such as occur and leaves it to be disentangled and evolved by those who have more leisure to bestow upon it.

Not that always where the language is intricate the thought is subtle, or the image always great where the line is bulky; the equality of words to things is very often neglected, and trivial sentiments and vulgar ideas disappoint the attention to which they are recommended by sonorous epithets and swelling figures.

But the admirers of this great poet have most reason to complain when he approaches nearest to his highest excellence and seems fully resolved [1] to sink them in dejection and mollify them with tender emotions by the fall of greatness, the danger of innocence, or the crosses of love. What he does best, he soon ceases to do. [2] He is not long soft and pathetic without some idle conceit or contemptible equivocation. He no sooner begins to move than he counteracts himself; and terror and pity, as they are rising in the mind, are checked and blasted by sudden frigidity.

A quibble is to Shakespeare what luminous vapors are to

[1] The opening phrase of this sentence assumed its present form in 1778. It originally read: "But the admirers of this great poet have never less reason to indulge their hopes of supreme excellence than when he seems fully resolved," etc. The difficulty of the sentence seems to arise mainly from the phrase "sink them in dejection," which in Johnson's critical vocabulary refers to one of Shakespeare's highest excellencies and not, as a hasty reader might think, to a form of disappointment with Shakespeare.

[2] This sentence is added in 1778.

the traveler; he follows it at all adventures; it is sure to lead him out of his way and sure to engulf him in the mire. It has some malignant power over his mind, and its fascinations are irresistible. Whatever be the dignity or profundity of his disquisition, whether he be enlarging knowledge or exalting affection, whether he be amusing attention with incidents or enchaining it in suspense, let but a quibble spring up before him, and he leaves his work unfinished. A quibble is the golden apple for which he will always turn aside from his career or stoop from his elevation. A quibble, poor and barren as it is, gave him such delight that he was content to purchase it by the sacrifice of reason, propriety, and truth. A quibble was to him the fatal Cleopatra for which he lost the world and was content to lose it.

It will be thought strange that in enumerating the defects of this writer I have not yet mentioned his neglect of the unities, his violation of those laws which have been instituted and established by the joint authority of poets and critics.

For his other deviations from the art of writing, I resign him to critical justice, without making any other demand in his favor than that which must be indulged to all human excellence: that his virtues be rated with his failings. But from the censure which this irregularity may bring upon him, I shall, with due reverence to that learning which I must oppose, adventure to try how I can defend him.

His histories, being neither tragedies nor comedies, are not subject to any of their laws; nothing more is necessary to all the praise which they expect than that the changes of action be so prepared as to be understood, that the incidents be various and affecting, and the characters consistent, natural, and distinct. No other unity is intended, and therefore none is to be sought.

In his other works he has well enough preserved the unity of action. He has not, indeed, an intrigue regularly perplexed and regularly unraveled; he does not endeavor to hide his design only to discover it, for this is seldom the order of real events, and Shakespeare is the poet of nature; but his plan has commonly, what Aristotle requires, a beginning, a middle, and an end; one event is concatenated with another, and the conclusion follows by easy consequence. There are perhaps some incidents that might be

spared, as in other poets there is much talk that only fills
up time upon the stage; but the general system makes gradual advances, and the end of the play is the end of expectation.

To the unities of time and place he has shown no regard; and perhaps a nearer view of the principles on which
they stand will diminish their value and withdraw from
them the veneration which, from the time of Corneille,[1]
they have very generally received, by discovering that they
have given more trouble to the poet than pleasure to the
auditor.

The necessity of observing the unities of time and place
arises from the supposed necessity of making the drama
credible. The critics hold it impossible that an action of
months or years can be possibly believed to pass in three
hours; or that the spectator can suppose himself to sit in
the theater while ambassadors go and return between distant kings, while armies are levied and towns besieged,
while an exile wanders and returns, or till he whom they
saw courting his mistress shall lament the untimely fall of
his son. The mind revolts from evident falsehood, and
fiction loses its force when it departs from the resemblance of reality.

From the narrow limitation of time necessarily arises
the contraction of place. The spectator, who knows that
he saw the first act at Alexandria, cannot suppose that he
sees the next at Rome, at a distance to which not the
dragons of Medea could, in so short a time, have transported him; he knows with certainty that he has not
changed his place; and he knows that place cannot change
itself; that what was a house cannot become a plain; that
what was Thebes can never be Persepolis.

Such is the triumphant language with which a critic
exults over the misery of an irregular poet and exults commonly without resistance or reply. It is time, therefore, to
tell him by the authority of Shakespeare, that he assumes,
as an unquestionable principle, a position which, while

---

[1] In the edition of his works published in 1660 Corneille
prefixed an *Examen* to each play and included also three *Discours* on the drama. In the third of these, the *Discours des
trois unités, d'action, de jour, et de lieu,* and in the *Examens*
he discusses the supposedly Aristotelian unities which had de-
veloped from the criticism of such Italians as Scaliger (1561)
and Castelvetro (1570).

his breath is forming it into words, his understanding pronounces to be false. It is false, that any representation
is mistaken for reality; that any dramatic fable in its mate-
riality was ever credible, or, for a single moment, was
ever credited.

The objection arising from the impossibility of passing
the first hour at Alexandria and the next at Rome, supposes that when the play opens the spectator really imagines himself at Alexandria and believes that his walk to
the theater has been a voyage to Egypt, and that he lives
in the days of Antony and Cleopatra. Surely he that imagines this may imagine more. He that can take the stage at
one time for the palace of the Ptolemies may take it in
half an hour for the promontory of Actium. Delusion, if
delusion be admitted, has no certain limitation; if the
spectator can be once persuaded that his old acquaintance [1] are Alexander and Caesar, that a room illuminated
with candles is the plain of Pharsalia or the bank of Granicus, he is in a state of elevation above the reach of reason or of truth, and from the heights of empyrean poetry
may despise the circumscriptions of terrestrial nature.
There is no reason why a mind thus wandering in ecstasy
should count the clock, or why an hour should not be a
century in that calenture of the brains that can make the
stage a field.

The truth is that the spectators are always in their senses
and know, from the first act to the last that the stage is
only a stage, and that the players are only players. They
come to hear a certain number of lines recited with just
gesture and elegant modulation. The lines relate to some
action, and an action must be in some place; but the different actions that complete a story may be in places very remote from each other; and where is the absurdity of al-
lowing that space to represent first Athens and then Sicily
which was always known to be neither Sicily nor Athens,
but a modern theater.

[1] Boswell gives us the following condensed note of a Johnsonian conversation in London on May 9, 1772: "No tragedy is
so strong on stage as alone. The effect all imagi[nation], and
when alone, nothing to counteract it; whereas in playhouse,
see 'tis stage, not wild heath; Garrick, not Macbeth" (from *Private Papers of James Boswell from Malahide Castle in the
Collection of Lt.-Colonel Ralph Heyward Isham*, IX, ed. Frederick A. Pottle [1930], 265. Reprinted by permission of Yale
University and McGraw-Hill Book Company, Inc.).

By supposition, as place is introduced, time may be extended; the time required by the fable elapses for the most part between the acts; for, of so much of the action as is represented, the real and poetical duration is the same. If in the first act preparations for war against Mithridates are represented to be made in Rome, the event of the war may, without absurdity, be represented in the catastrophe as happening in Pontus; we know that there is neither war nor preparation for war; we know that we are neither in Rome nor Pontus; that neither Mithridates nor Lucullus are before us. The drama exhibits successive imitations of successive actions; and why may not the second imitation represent an action that happened years after the first, if it be so connected with it that nothing but time can be supposed to intervene? Time is, of all modes of existence, most obsequious to the imagination; a lapse of years is as easily conceived as a passage of hours. In contemplation we easily contract the time of real actions and therefore willingly permit it to be contracted when we only see their imitation.

It will be asked how the drama moves if it is not credited. It is credited with all the credit due to a drama. It is credited, whenever it moves, as a just picture of a real original; as representing to the auditor what he would himself feel if he were to do or suffer what is there feigned to be suffered or to be done. The reflection that strikes the heart is not that the evils before us are real evils, but that they are evils to which we ourselves may be exposed. If there be any fallacy, it is not that we fancy the players, but that we fancy ourselves unhappy for a moment; but we rather lament the possibility than suppose the presence of misery, as a mother weeps over her babe when she remembers that death may take it from her. The delight of tragedy proceeds from our consciousness of fiction; if we thought murders and treasons real, they would please no more.

Imitations produce pain or pleasure, not because they are mistaken for realities, but because they bring realities to mind. When the imagination is recreated by a painted landscape, the trees are not supposed capable to give us shade, or the fountains coolness; but we consider how we should be pleased with such fountains playing beside us and such woods waving over us. We are agitated in reading the history of *Henry the Fifth*, yet no man takes his book for the field of Agincourt. A dramatic exhibition is a book recited with concomitants that increase or diminish its effect. Familiar comedy is often more powerful in the theater than on the page; imperial tragedy is always less. The humor of Petruchio may be heightened by grimace; but what voice or what gesture can hope to add dignity or force to the soliloquy of Cato? [1]

A play read affects the mind like a play acted. It is therefore evident that the action is not supposed to be real; and it follows that between the acts a longer or shorter time may be allowed to pass, and that no more account of space or duration is to be taken by the auditor of a drama than by the reader of a narrative, before whom may pass in an hour the life of a hero or the revolutions of an empire.

Whether Shakespeare knew the unities and rejected them by design, or deviated from them by happy ignorance, it is, I think, impossible to decide and useless to inquire. We may reasonably suppose that, when he rose to notice, he did not want the counsels and admonitions of scholars and critics, and that he at last deliberately persisted in a practice, which he might have begun by chance. As nothing is essential to the fable but unity of action, and as the unities of time and place arise evidently from false assumptions, and, by circumscribing the extent of the drama, lessen its variety, I cannot think it much to be lamented that they were not known by him, or not observed; nor, if such another poet could arise, should I very vehemently reproach him that his first act passed at Venice and his next in Cyprus.[2] Such violations of rules merely positive become the comprehensive genius of Shakespeare, and such censures are suitable to the minute and slender criticism of Voltaire:

> Non usque adeo permiscuit imis
> Longus summa dies, ut non, si voce Metelli
> Serventur leges, malint a Caesare tolli.[3]

Yet when I speak thus slightly of dramatic rules, I cannot but recollect how much wit and learning may be pro-

---

[1] Addison, *Cato,* V. i.   [2] *Othello,* Acts I and II.
[3] Lucan, *Pharsalia,* III. 138–140: in the translation by J. D. Duff, "The course of time has not wrought such confusion that the laws would not rather be trampled on by Caesar than saved by Metellus."

duced against me; before such authorities I am afraid to stand, not that I think the present question one of those that are to be decided by mere authority, but because it is to be suspected that these precepts have not been so easily received but for better reasons than I have yet been able to find. The result of my inquiries, in which it would be ludicrous to boast of impartiality, is that the unities of time and place are not essential to a just drama; that, though they may sometimes conduce to pleasure, they are always to be sacrificed to the nobler beauties of variety and instruction; and that a play written with nice observation of critical rules is to be contemplated as an elaborate curiosity, as the product of superfluous and ostentatious art, by which is shown, rather what is possible, than what is necessary.

He that, without diminution of any other excellence, shall preserve all the unities unbroken deserves the like applause with the architect who shall display all the orders of architecture in a citadel without any deduction from its strength; but the principal beauty of a citadel is to exclude the enemy, and the greatest graces of a play are to copy nature and instruct life.

Perhaps what I have here not dogmatically but deliberatively written may recall the principles of the drama to a new examination. I am almost frighted at my own temerity and, when I estimate the fame and the strength of those that maintain the contrary opinion, am ready to sink down in reverential silence; as Aeneas withdrew from the defense of Troy when he saw Neptune shaking the wall and Juno heading the besiegers.[1]

Those whom my arguments cannot persuade to give their approbation to the judgment of Shakespeare will easily, if they consider the condition of his life, make some allowance for his ignorance.

Every man's performances, to be rightly estimated, must be compared with the state of the age in which he lived and with his own particular opportunities; and though to a reader a book be not worse or better for the circumstances of the author, yet as there is always a silent reference of human works to human abilities, and as the inquiry how far man may extend his designs, or how high he may rate his native force, is of far greater dignity than in what rank we

[1] *Aeneid,* II. 610–614.

shall place any particular performance, curiosity is always busy to discover the instruments as well as to survey the workmanship, to know how much is to be ascribed to original powers and how much to casual and adventitious help. The palaces of Peru or Mexico were certainly mean and incommodious habitations if compared to the houses of European monarchs; yet who could forbear to view them with astonishment who remembered that they were built without the use of iron?

The English nation, in the time of Shakespeare, was yet struggling to emerge from barbarity. The philology of Italy had been transplanted hither in the reign of Henry the Eighth; and the learned languages had been successfully cultivated by Lily, Linacre, and More; by Pole, Cheke, and Gardiner; [1] and afterwards by Smith, Clerk, Haddon, and Ascham.[2] Greek was now taught to boys in the principal schools; and those who united elegance with learning read with great diligence the Italian and Spanish poets. But literature was yet confined to professed scholars, or to men and women of high rank. The public was gross and dark; and to be able to read and write was an accomplishment still valued for its rarity.

Nations, like individuals, have their infancy. A people newly awakened to literary curiosity, being yet unacquainted with the true state of things, knows not how to judge of that which is proposed as its resemblance. Whatever is remote from common appearances is always welcome to vulgar, as to childish, credulity; and of a country unenlightened by learning, the whole people is the vulgar. The study of those who then aspired to plebeian learning

[1] A roster of Tudor humanists and scholars: William Lily wrote a Latin grammar which was used by Shakespeare. Thomas Linacre and Sir John Cheke were teachers of Greek, at Oxford and Cambridge respectively. Stephen Gardiner and Reginald Pole were churchmen and chancellors of Cambridge University. Sir Thomas More, Henry VIII's Chancellor, is best known to the world of letters as the author of the sophisticated Latin work *Utopia*.

[2] Sir Thomas Smith and Walter Haddon were regius professors of civil law and vice-chancellors of Cambridge University. John Clerk was Bishop of Bath and Wells. Roger Ascham was Latin secretary to Queen Mary, private tutor to Queen Elizabeth, and author of *Toxophilus* and *The Schoolmaster*.

was laid out upon adventures, giants, dragons, and enchantments. *The Death of Arthur* was the favorite volume.[1]

The mind which has feasted on the luxurious wonders of fiction has no taste for the insipidity of truth. A play which imitated only the common occurrences of the world would, upon the admirers of *Palmerin* and *Guy of Warwick*,[2] have made little impression; he that wrote for such an audience was under the necessity of looking round for strange events and fabulous transactions; and that incredibility by which maturer knowledge is offended was the chief recommendation of writings to unskillful curiosity.

Our author's plots are generally borrowed from novels; and it is reasonable to suppose that he chose the most popular, such as were read by many and related by more; for his audience could not have followed him through the intricacies of the drama, had they not held the thread of the story in their hands.

The stories which we now find only in remoter authors were in his time accessible and familiar. The fable of *As You Like It*, which is supposed to be copied from Chaucer's *Gamelyn*, was a little pamphlet of those times; [3] and old Mr. Cibber [4] remembered the tale of *Hamlet* in plain English prose, which the critics have now to seek in Saxo Grammaticus.[5]

---

[1] Sir Thomas Malory's *Morte d'Arthur* was published by Caxton in 1485.

[2] *Palmerin D'Oliva* and *Palmerin of England* were Spanish prose romances translated into English by Anthony Munday in 1588 and 1596. Johnson tried an Italian version of the latter in 1776 but "did not like it much." He was said to have been as a boy "immoderately fond of reading romances of chivalry" (Boswell, *Life*, I. 49; III. 2). *Guy of Warwick* was an English verse romance written about 1308 and published by Pynson early in the sixteenth century.

[3] The *Tale of Gamelyn* was rejected from the Chaucer canon by Tyrwhitt in 1775. It was a predecessor of Thomas Lodge's *Rosalynde* (1590), which was the immediate source of Shakespeare's *As You Like It*. D. N. Smith, 1928, p. 51, suggests that Johnson withheld the name of the "pamphlet" in order not to take credit from the actual discoverer, his friend Richard Farmer of Cambridge, who in 1767 was to publish his *Essay on the Learning of Shakespeare*.

[4] Colley Cibber, actor and dramatist, Poet Laureate in 1730.

[5] Danish historian (c. 1150–1206), author of *Gesta Danorum*, or *Historia Danica*, printed at Paris in 1514, translated from the Latin into Danish in 1575.

His English histories he took from English chronicles and English ballads; and as the ancient writers were made known to his countrymen by versions, they supplied him with new subjects; he dilated some of Plutarch's lives into plays, when they had been translated by North.[1]

His plots, whether historical or fabulous, are always crowded with incidents, by which the attention of a rude people was more easily caught than by sentiment or argumentation; and such is the power of the marvelous, even over those who despise it, that every man finds his mind more strongly seized by the tragedies of Shakespeare than of any other writer. Others please us by particular speeches; but he always makes us anxious for the event and has perhaps excelled all but Homer in securing the first purpose of a writer, by exciting restless and unquenchable curiosity and compelling him that reads his work to read it through.

The shows and bustle with which his plays abound have the same original. As knowledge advances, pleasure passes from the eye to the ear, but returns, as it declines, from the ear to the eye. Those to whom our author's labors were exhibited had more skill in pomps or processions than in poetical language and perhaps wanted some visible and discriminated events as comments on the dialogue. He knew how he should most please; and whether his practice is more agreeable to nature, or whether his example has prejudiced the nation, we still find that on our stage something must be done as well as said, and inactive declamation is very coldly heard, however musical or elegant, passionate or sublime.

Voltaire expresses his wonder that our author's extravagances are endured by a nation which has seen the tragedy of *Cato*.[2] Let him be answered that Addison speaks the language of poets; and Shakespeare, of men. We find in *Cato* innumerable beauties which enamor us of its author, but we see nothing that acquaints us with human sentiments or human actions; we place it with the fairest and the noblest progeny which judgment propagates by conjunction with learning; but *Othello* is the vigorous and vivacious off-

[1] Sir Thomas North published the first edition of his translation of Plutarch's *Lives of the Noble Grecians and Romans,* from the French of Amyot, in 1579.
[2] *L'Appel* (*Oeuvres,* ed. Moland, XXIV, 201).

spring of observation impregnated by genius. *Cato* affords a splendid exhibition of artificial and fictitious manners and delivers just and noble sentiments, in diction easy, elevated, and harmonious, but its hopes and fears communicate no vibration to the heart; the composition refers us only to the writer; we pronounce the name of *Cato,* but we think on Addison.

The work of a correct and regular writer is a garden accurately formed and diligently planted, varied with shades, and scented with flowers; the composition of Shakespeare is a forest, in which oaks extend their branches, and pines tower in the air, interspersed sometimes with weeds and brambles, and sometimes giving shelter to myrtles and to roses; filling the eye with awful pomp and gratifying the mind with endless diversity. Other poets display cabinets of precious rarities, minutely finished, wrought into shape, and polished into brightness. Shakespeare opens a mine which contains gold and diamonds in unexhaustible plenty, though clouded by incrustations, debased by impurities, and mingled with a mass of meaner minerals.

It has been much disputed whether Shakespeare owed his excellence to his own native force, or whether he had the common helps of scholastic education, the precepts of critical science, and the examples of ancient authors.

There has always prevailed a tradition that Shakespeare wanted learning, that he had no regular education, nor much skill in the dead languages. Jonson, his friend, affirms that *he had small Latin, and less* [1] *Greek;* who, besides that he had no imaginable temptation to falsehood, wrote at a time when the character and acquisitions of Shakespeare were known to multitudes. His evidence ought therefore to decide the controversy, unless some testimony of equal force could be opposed.

Some have imagined that they have discovered deep learning in many imitations of old writers; but the examples which I have known urged were drawn from books translated in his time; or were such easy coincidences of thought as will happen to all who consider the same subjects; or such remarks on life or axioms of morality as float in con-

[1] 1765 has "no Greek," corrected to "less Greek" in 1773, the true reading of Ben Jonson's verses "To the Memory of My Beloved . . . Mr. William Shakespeare," prefixed to the First Folio.

versation and are transmitted through the world in proverbial sentences.

I have found it remarked that in this important sentence, *Go before, I'll follow,* we read a translation of, *I prae, sequar.*[1] I have been told that when Caliban, after a pleasing dream, says, *I cried to sleep again,*[2] the author imitates Anacreon, who had, like every other man, the same wish on the same occasion.

There are a few passages which may pass for imitations, but so few that the exception only confirms the rule; he obtained them from accidental quotations or by oral communication and, as he used what he had, would have used more if he had obtained it.

The *Comedy of Errors* is confessedly taken from the *Menaechmi* of Plautus; from the only play of Plautus which was then in English. What can be more probable than that he who copied that would have copied more; but that those which were not translated were inaccessible?

Whether he knew the modern languages is uncertain. That his plays have some French scenes proves but little; he might easily procure them to be written, and probably, even though he had known the language in the common degree, he could not have written it without assistance. In the story of *Romeo and Juliet* he is observed to have followed the English translation, where it deviates from the Italian; but this on the other part proves nothing against his knowledge of the original. He was to copy, not what he knew himself, but what was known to his audience.

It is most likely that he had learned Latin sufficiently to make him acquainted with construction, but that he never advanced to an easy perusal of the Roman authors. Concerning his skill in modern languages, I can find no sufficient ground of determination; but as no imitations of French or Italian authors have been discovered, though the Italian poetry was then high in esteem, I am inclined to believe that he read little more than English and chose for his fables only such tales as he found translated.

That much knowledge is scattered over his works is very justly observed by Pope; but it is often such knowledge as

---

[1] Zachary Grey, *Critical, Historical, and Explanatory Notes on Shakespeare* (1754), II, 53. (See Sherbo, pp. 41–42). Grey compared *Richard III,* I. i. 143 to Terence, *Andria,* 1. 171.

[2] *Tempest,* III. ii. 155: "I cried to dream again."

books did not supply. He that will understand Shakespeare must not be content to study him in the closet, he must look for his meaning sometimes among the sports of the field and sometimes among the manufactures of the shop.

There is, however, proof enough that he was a very diligent reader, nor was our language then so indigent of books but that he might very liberally indulge his curiosity without excursion into foreign literature. Many of the Roman authors were translated, and some of the Greek; the Reformation had filled the kingdom with theological learning; most of the topics of human disquisition had found English writers; and poetry had been cultivated not only with diligence but success. This was a stock of knowledge sufficient for a mind so capable of appropriating and improving it.

But the greater part of his excellence was the product of his own genius. He found the English stage in a state of the utmost rudeness; no essays either in tragedy or comedy had appeared from which it could be discovered to what degree of delight either one or other might be carried. Neither character nor dialogue were yet understood. Shakespeare may be truly said to have introduced them both amongst us and in some of his happier scenes to have carried them both to the utmost height.

By what gradations of improvement he proceeded is not easily known; for the chronology of his works is yet unsettled. Rowe is of opinion that " perhaps we are not to look for his beginning, like those of other writers, in his least perfect works; art had so little and nature so large a share in what he did, that for aught I know," says he, "the performances of his youth, as they were the most vigorous, were the best." [1] But the power of nature is only the power of using to any certain purpose the materials which diligence procures or opportunity supplies. Nature gives no man knowledge, and, when images are collected by study and experience, can only assist in combining or applying them. Shakespeare, however favored by nature, could impart only what he had learned; and as he must increase his ideas, like other mortals, by gradual acquisition, he, like them, grew wiser as he grew older, could display

[1] Rowe's *Some Account of the Life of Mr. William Shakespeare,* prefixed to his edition of 1709, pp. VI–VII (Augustan Reprint Society facsimile, 1948), quoted with variations.

life better, as he knew it more, and instruct with more efficacy, as he was himself more amply instructed.

There is a vigilance of observation and accuracy of distinction which books and precepts cannot confer; from this almost all original and native excellence proceeds. Shakespeare must have looked upon mankind with perspicacity, in the highest degree curious and attentive. Other writers borrow their characters from preceding writers and diversify them only by the accidental appendages of present manners; the dress is a little varied, but the body is the same. Our author had both matter and form to provide; for, except the characters of Chaucer, to whom I think he is not much indebted, there were no writers in English, and perhaps not many in other modern languages, which showed life in its native colors.

The contest about the original benevolence or malignity of man had not yet commenced. Speculation had not yet attempted to analyze the mind, to trace the passions to their sources, to unfold the seminal principles of vice and virtue, or sound the depths of the heart for the motives of action. All those inquiries, which from that time that human nature became the fashionable study have been made sometimes with nice discernment but often with idle subtilty, were yet unattempted. The tales with which the infancy of learning was satisfied exhibited only the superficial appearances of action, related the events but omitted the causes, and were formed for such as delighted in wonders rather than in truth. Mankind was not then to be studied in the closet; he that would know the world was under the necessity of gleaning his own remarks by mingling as he could in its business and amusements.

Boyle congratulated himself upon his high birth, because it favored his curiosity by facilitating his access.[1] Shakespeare had no such advantage; he came to London a needy adventurer and lived for a time by very mean employments. Many works of genius and learning have been performed in states of life that appear very little favorable to thought or to inquiry; so many that he who considers them is inclined to think that he sees enterprise and perseverance predominating over all external agency and bidding help and hindrance vanish before them. The genius

[1] Thomas Birch, *Life of the Hon. Robert Boyle* (1744), pp. 18–19.

of Shakespeare was not to be depressed by the weight of
poverty nor limited by the narrow conversation to which
men in want are inevitably condemned; the incumbrances
of his fortune were shaken from his mind, *as dew-drops
from a lion's mane.*[1]

Though he had so many difficulties to encounter and so
little assistance to surmount them, he has been able to obtain an exact knowledge of many modes of life and many
casts of native dispositions, to vary them with great multiplicity, to mark them by nice distinctions, and to show
them in full view by proper combinations. In this part of
his performances he had none to imitate, but has himself
been imitated by all succeeding writers; and it may be
doubted whether from all his successors more maxims of
theoretical knowledge or more rules of practical prudence
can be collected than he alone has given to his country.

Nor was his attention confined to the actions of men;
he was an exact surveyor of the inanimate world; his descriptions have always some peculiarities gathered by con-
templating things as they really exist. It may be observed
that the oldest poets of many nations preserve their reputation, and that the following generations of wit, after a
short celebrity, sink into oblivion. The first, whoever they
may be, must take their sentiments and descriptions immediately from knowledge; the resemblance is therefore
just, their descriptions are verified by every eye, and their
sentiments acknowledged by every breast. Those whom
their fame invites to the same studies copy partly them and
partly nature, till the books of one age gain such authority
as to stand in the place of nature to another, and imitation,
always deviating a little, becomes at last capricious and
casual. Shakespeare, whether life or nature be his subject,
shows plainly that he has seen with his own eyes; he gives
the image which he receives, not weakened or distorted
by the intervention of any other mind; the ignorant feel
his representations to be just, and the learned see that they
are complete.

Perhaps it would not be easy to find any author, except
Homer, who invented so much as Shakespeare, who so
much advanced the studies which he cultivated or effused
so much novelty upon his age or country. The form, the
characters, the language, and the shows of the English

[1] *Troilus and Cressida,* III. iii. 225.

drama are his. "He seems," says Dennis, "to have been the very original of our English tragical harmony, that is, the harmony of blank verse, diversified often by dissyllable and trisyllable terminations. For the diversity distinguishes it from heroic harmony, and by bringing it nearer to common use makes it more proper to gain attention and more fit for action and dialogue. Such verse we make when we are writing prose; we make such verse in common conversation." [1]

I know not whether this praise is rigorously just. The dissyllable termination, which the critic rightly appropriates to the drama, is to be found—though, I think, not in *Gorboduc,* which is confessedly before our author—yet in *Hieronimo,*[2] of which the date is not certain, but which there is reason to believe at least as old as his earliest plays. This, however, is certain, that he is the first who taught either tragedy or comedy to please, there being no theatrical piece of any older writer of which the name is known except to antiquaries and collectors of books which are sought because they are scarce, and would not have been scarce, had they been much esteemed.

To him we must ascribe the praise, unless Spenser may divide it with him, of having first discovered to how much smoothness and harmony the English language could be softened. He has speeches, perhaps sometimes scenes, which have all the delicacy of Rowe, without his effeminacy. He endeavors indeed commonly to strike by the force and vigor of his dialogue, but he never executes his purpose better than when he tries to soothe by softness.

Yet it must be at last confessed that as we owe everything to him, he owes something to us; that, if much of his praise is paid by perception and judgment, much is likewise given by custom and veneration. We fix our eyes upon his graces and turn them from his deformities and endure in him what we should in another loathe and despise. If we endured without praising, respect for the father of our drama might excuse us; but I have seen in the book of some modern critic [3] a collection of anomalies, which show

[1] *An Essay on the Genius and Writings of Shakespeare,* 1712 (*Works,* ed. Hooker, II, 45), with slight variations.

[2] Thomas Kyd's *Spanish Tragedy or Hieronimo Is Mad Again* was acted first in 1592 and printed in the same year or shortly after.

[3] John Upton, *Critical Observations on Shakespeare,* 1746, 1748. (*Cf.* Sherbo, pp. 42, 52–53.)

that he has corrupted language by every mode of depravation, but which his admirer has accumulated as a monument of honor.

He has scenes of undoubted and perpetual excellence; but perhaps not one play which, if it were now exhibited as the work of a contemporary writer, would be heard to the conclusion. I am indeed far from thinking that his works were wrought to his own ideas of perfection; when they were such as would satisfy the audience, they satisfied the writer. It is seldom that authors, though more studious of fame than Shakespeare, rise much above the standard of their own age; to add a little to what is best will always be sufficient for present praise, and those who find themselves exalted into fame are willing to credit their encomiasts and to spare the labor of contending with themselves.

It does not appear that Shakespeare thought his works worthy of posterity, that he levied any ideal tribute upon future times, or had any further prospect than of present popularity and present profit. When his plays had been acted, his hope was at an end; he solicited no addition of honor from the reader. He therefore made no scruple to repeat the same jests in many dialogues, or to entangle different plots by the same knot of perplexity, which may at least be forgiven him by those who recollect that of Congreve's four comedies two are concluded by a marriage in a mask, by a deception which perhaps never happened, and which, whether likely or not, he did not invent.

So careless was this great poet of future fame that, though he retired to ease and plenty while he was yet little *declined into the vale of years,*[1] before he could be disgusted with fatigue or disabled by infirmity, he made no collection of his works nor desired to rescue those that had been already published from the depravations that obscured them or secure to the rest a better destiny, by giving them to the world in their genuine state.

Of the plays which bear the name of Shakespeare in the late editions, the greater part were not published till about seven years after his death; and the few which appeared in his life are apparently thrust into the world without the care of the author and therefore probably without his knowledge.

Of all the publishers, clandestine or professed, the [2] neg-

[1] *Othello,* III. iii. 265.
[2] 1765 has "their," corrected to "the" in 1780.

ligence and unskillfulness has by the late revisers been sufficiently shown. The faults of all are indeed numerous
and gross and have not only corrupted many passages perhaps beyond recovery but have brought others into suspicion which are only obscured by obsolete phraseology
or by the writer's unskillfulness and affectation. To alter
is more easy than to explain, and temerity is a more common quality than diligence. Those who saw that they must
employ conjecture to a certain degree were willing to indulge it a little further. Had the author published his own
works, we should have sat quietly down to disentangle his
intricacies and clear his obscurities; but now we tear what
we cannot loose and eject what we happen not to understand.

The faults are more than could have happened without
the concurrence of many causes. The style of Shakespeare
was in itself ungrammatical, perplexed, and obscure; his
works were transcribed for the players by those who may
be supposed to have seldom understood them; they were
transmitted by copiers equally unskillful, who still multiplied errors; they were perhaps sometimes mutilated by the
actors, for the sake of shortening the speeches, and were
at last printed without correction of the press.

In this state they remained, not as Dr. Warburton supposes,[1] because they were unregarded, but because the editor's art was not yet applied to modern languages, and our
ancestors were accustomed to so much negligence of
English printers that they could very patiently endure it.
At last an edition was undertaken by Rowe; not because a
poet was to be published by a poet, for Rowe seems to have
thought very little on correction or explanation; but that
our author's works might appear like those of his frater-
nity, with the appendages of a life and recommendatory
preface. Rowe has been clamorously blamed for not per-
forming what he did not undertake; and it is time that
justice be done him, by confessing that though he seems
to have had no thought of corruption beyond the printer's
errors, yet he has made many emendations, if they were
not made before, which his successors have received with-

[1] Warburton's *Preface*, 1747: "The stubborn nonsense with
which he was encrusted occasioned his lying long neglected
amongst the common lumber of the stage" (¶ 2, in Johnson-
Steevens edition, 1773).

out acknowledgment, and which, if they had produced them, would have filled pages and pages with censures of the stupidity by which the faults were committed, with displays of the absurdities which they involved, with ostentatious expositions of the new reading, and self-congratulations on the happiness of discovering it.

As of the other editors I have preserved the prefaces, I have likewise borrowed the author's life from Rowe,[1] though not written with much elegance or spirit; it relates, however, what is now to be known, and therefore deserves to pass through all succeeding publications.

The nation had been for many years content enough with Mr. Rowe's performance, when Mr. Pope made them acquainted with the true state of Shakespeare's text, showed that it was extremely corrupt, and gave reason to hope that there were means of reforming it. He collated the old copies, which none had thought to examine before, and restored many lines to their integrity; but, by a very compendious criticism, he rejected whatever he disliked and thought more of amputation than of cure.

I know not why he is commended by Dr. Warburton for distinguishing the genuine from the spurious plays.[2] In his choice he exerted no judgment of his own; the plays which he received were given by Heming and Condell, the first editors; and those which he rejected, though, according to the licentiousness of the press in those times, they were printed during Shakespeare's life, with his name, had been omitted by his friends and were never added to his works before the edition of 1664, from which they were copied by the later printers.

This was a work which Pope seems to have thought unworthy of his abilities, being not able to suppress his contempt of *the dull duty of an editor*.[3] He understood but half his undertaking. The duty of a collator is indeed dull, yet, like other tedious tasks, is very necessary; but an emend-

---

[1] 1765: "Of Rowe, as of all the editors, I have preserved the preface, and have likewise retained the author's life. . . ." The revision is made in 1773.

[2] *Preface*, 1747 (¶ 4 in 1773).

[3] "I have discharged the dull duty of an editor, to my best judgment, with more labor than I expect thanks, with a religious abhorrence of all innovation, and without any indulgence to my private sense or conjecture" (Pope's *Preface*, 1725, next to last paragraph).

atory critic would ill discharge his duty without qualities very different from dullness. In perusing a corrupted piece, he must have before him all possibilities of meaning, with all possibilities of expression. Such must be his comprehension of thought and such his copiousness of language. Out of many readings possible, he must be able to select that which best suits with the state, opinions, and modes of language prevailing in every age and with his author's particular cast of thought and turn of expression. Such must be his knowledge and such his taste. Conjectural criticism demands more than humanity possesses, and he that exercises it with most praise has very frequent need of indulgence. Let us now be told no more of the dull duty of an editor.

Confidence is the common consequence of success. They whose excellence of any kind has been loudly celebrated are ready to conclude that their powers are universal. Pope's edition fell below his own expectations, and he was so much offended when he was found to have left anything for others to do that he passed the latter part of his life in a state of hostility with verbal criticism.

I have retained all his notes, that no fragment of so great a writer may be lost. His Preface, valuable alike for elegance of composition and justness of remark, and containing a general criticism on his author so extensive that little can be added and so exact that little can be disputed, every editor has an interest to suppress, but that every reader would demand its insertion.

Pope was succeeded by Theobald, a man of narrow comprehension and small acquisitions, with no native and intrinsic splendor of genius, with little of the artificial light of learning, but zealous for minute accuracy and not negligent in pursuing it. He collated the ancient copies and rectified many errors. A man so anxiously scrupulous might have been expected to do more, but what little he did was commonly right.

In his reports of copies and editions he is not to be trusted without examination. He speaks sometimes indefinitely of copies, when he has only one. In his enumeration of editions, he mentions the two first folios as of high, and the third folio as of middle authority; but the truth is that the first is equivalent to all others, and that the rest only deviate from it by the printer's negligence.

Whoever has any of the folios has all, excepting those
diversities which mere reiteration of editions will produce. I collated them all at the beginning, but afterwards
used only the first.

Of his notes I have generally retained those which he
retained himself in his second edition, except when they
were confuted by subsequent annotators or were too minute
to merit preservation. I have sometimes adopted his restoration of a comma, without inserting the panegyric in which
he celebrated himself for his achievement. The exuberant
excrescence of his diction I have often lopped, his triumphant exultations over Pope and Rowe I have sometimes
suppressed, and his contemptible ostentation I have frequently concealed; but I have in some places shown him,
as he would have shown himself, for the reader's diversion,
that the inflated emptiness of some notes may justify or
excuse the contraction of the rest.

Theobald, thus weak and ignorant, thus mean and faith-
less, thus petulant and ostentatious, by the good luck of
having Pope for his enemy, has escaped, and escaped alone,
with reputation, from this undertaking. So willingly does
the world support those who solicit favor, against those
who command reverence; and so easily is he praised whom
no man can envy.

Our author fell then into the hands of Sir Thomas
Hanmer, the Oxford editor, a man, in my opinion, eminently qualified by nature for such studies. He had, what
is the first requisite to emendatory criticism, that intuition
by which the poet's intention is immediately discovered,
and that dexterity of intellect which dispatches its work
by the easiest means. He had undoubtedly read much; his
acquaintance with customs, opinions, and traditions,
seems to have been large; and he is often learned without
show. He seldom passes what he does not understand,
without an attempt to find or to make a meaning, and
sometimes hastily makes what a little more attention would
have found. He is solicitous to reduce to grammar what he
could not be sure that his author intended to be grammatical. Shakespeare regarded more the series of ideas than of
words; and his language, not being designed for the reader's
desk, was all that he desired it to be if it conveyed his
meaning to the audience.

Hanmer's care of the meter has been too violently censured. He found the measures reformed in so many passages by the silent labors of some editors, with the silent acquiescence of the rest, that he thought himself allowed to extend a little further the license which had already been carried so far without reprehension; and of his corrections in general, it must be confessed that they are often just, and made commonly with the least possible violation of the text.

But by inserting his emendations, whether invented or borrowed, into the page without any notice of varying copies, he has appropriated the labor of his predecessors and made his own edition of little authority. His confidence indeed, both in himself and others, was too great; he supposes all to be right that was done by Pope and Theobald; he seems not to suspect a critic of fallibility; and it was but reasonable that he should claim what he so liberally granted.

As he never writes without careful inquiry and diligent consideration, I have received all his notes and believe that every reader will wish for more.

Of the last editor [1] it is more difficult to speak. Respect is due to high place, tenderness to living reputation, and veneration to genius and learning; but he cannot be justly offended at that liberty of which he has himself so frequently given an example, nor very solicitous what is thought of notes which he ought never to have considered as part of his serious employments, and which, I suppose, since the ardor of composition is remitted, he no longer numbers among his happy effusions.

The original and predominant error of his commentary is acquiescence in his first thoughts; that precipitation which is produced by consciousness of quick discernment; and that confidence which presumes to do, by surveying the surface, what labor only can perform, by penetrating the bottom. His notes exhibit sometimes perverse interpretations and sometimes improbable conjectures; he at one time gives the author more profundity of meaning than the sentence admits and at another discovers absurdities where the sense is plain to every other reader. But his emendations are likewise often happy and just and his interpretation of obscure passages learned and sagacious.

Of his notes, I have commonly rejected those against
[1] Warburton, 1747.

which the general voice of the public has exclaimed, or which their own incongruity immediately condemns, and which, I suppose, the author himself would desire to be forgotten. Of the rest, to part I have given the highest approbation, by inserting the offered reading in the text; part I have left to the judgment of the reader, as doubtful, though specious; and part I have censured without reserve, but I am sure without bitterness of malice, and, I hope, without wantonness of insult.

It is no pleasure to me, in revising my volumes, to observe how much paper is wasted in confutation. Whoever considers the revolutions of learning and the various questions of greater or less importance upon which wit and reason have exercised their powers, must lament the unsuccessfulness of inquiry and the slow advances of truth, when he reflects that great part of the labor of every writer is only the destruction of those that went before him. The first care of the builder of a new system is to demolish the fabrics which are standing. The chief desire of him that comments an author is to show how much other commentators have corrupted and obscured him. The opinions prevalent in one age as truths above the reach of controversy are confuted and rejected in another and rise again to reception in remoter times. Thus the human mind is kept in motion without progress. Thus sometimes truth and error, and sometimes contrarieties of error, take each other's place by reciprocal invasion. The tide of seeming knowledge which is poured over one generation retires and leaves another naked and barren; the sudden meteors of intelligence which for a while appear to shoot their beams into the regions of obscurity, on a sudden withdraw their lustre and leave mortals again to grope their way.

These elevations and depressions of renown and the contradictions to which all improvers of knowledge must forever be exposed, since they are not escaped by the highest and brightest of mankind, may surely be endured with patience by critics and annotators, who can rank themselves but as the satellites of their authors. How canst thou beg for life, says Achilles [1] to his captive, when thou knowest that thou art now to suffer only what must another day be suffered by Achilles?

[1] 1773 substitutes for "Achilles" the periphrase "Homer's hero." Achilles to Lycaon, *Iliad*, XXI. 99ff.

Dr. Warburton had a name sufficient to confer celebrity on those who could exalt themselves into antagonists, and his notes have raised a clamor too loud to be distinct. His chief assailants are the authors of *The Canons of Criticism* and of the *Revival* [1] *of Shakespeare's Text;* of whom one ridicules his errors with airy petulance, suitable enough to the levity of the controversy; the other attacks them with gloomy malignity, as if he were dragging to justice an assassin or incendiary. The one stings like a fly, sucks a little blood, takes a gay flutter, and returns for more; the other bites like a viper and would be glad to leave inflammations and gangrene behind him. When I think on one, with his confederates, I remember the danger of Coriolanus, who was afraid that *girls with spits, and boys with stones, should slay him in puny battle;* [2] when the other crosses my imagination, I remember the prodigy in *Macbeth:*

> A falcon [3] towering in his pride of place,
> Was by a mousing owl hawk'd at and kill'd.

Let me, however, do them justice. One is a wit, and one a scholar. They have both shown acuteness sufficient in the discovery of faults and have both advanced some probable interpretations of obscure passages; but when they aspire to conjecture and emendation, it appears how falsely we all estimate our own abilities, and the little which they have been able to perform might have taught them more candor to the endeavors of others.

Before Dr. Warburton's edition, *Critical Observations on Shakespeare* had been published by Mr. Upton, [4] a man skilled in languages and acquainted with books, but who seems to have had no great vigor of genius or nicety of taste. Many of his explanations are curious and useful, but he, likewise, though he professed to oppose the licentious confidence of editors and adhere to the old copies, is unable to restrain the rage of emendation, though his ardor is ill seconded by his skill. Every cold empiric, when his

[1] 1765 has *"review,"* changed in 1778 to *"revisal."* The work in question is Benjamin Heath's *Revisal of Shakespeare's Text,* 1765. (See Sherbo, pp. 31–39.)

[2] *Coriolanus,* IV. iv. 5: ". . . Lest that thy wives with spits and boys with stones/ In puny battle slay me."

[3] 1765 has "eagle," corrected in 1773 to "falcon." *Macbeth,* II. iv. 12–13.

[4] See above, p. 50, n. 3.

heart is expanded by a successful experiment, swells into a theorist, and the laborious collator at some unlucky moment frolics in conjecture.

Critical, Historical, and Explanatory Notes have been likewise published upon Shakespeare by Dr. Grey,[1] whose diligent perusal of the old English writers has enabled him to make some useful observations. What he undertook he has well enough performed, but as he neither attempts judicial nor emendatory criticism, he employs rather his memory than his sagacity. It were to be wished that all would endeavor to imitate his modesty who have not been able to surpass his knowledge.

I can say with great sincerity of all my predecessors, what I hope will hereafter be said of me, that not one has left Shakespeare without improvement; nor is there one to whom I have not been indebted for assistance and information. Whatever I have taken from them, it was my intention to refer to its original author, and it is certain that what I have not given to another, I believed when I wrote it to be my own. In some perhaps I have been anticipated; but if I am ever found to encroach upon the remarks of any other commentator, I am willing that the honor, be it more or less, should be transferred to the first claimant, for his right, and his alone, stands above dispute; the second can prove his pretensions only to himself, nor can himself always distinguish invention, with sufficient certainty, from recollection.

They have all been treated by me with candor, which they have not been careful of observing to one another. It is not easy to discover from what cause the acrimony of a scholiast can naturally proceed. The subjects to be discussed by him are of very small importance; they involve neither property nor liberty, nor favor the interest of sect or party. The various readings of copies and different interpretations of a passage seem to be questions that might exercise the wit without engaging the passions. But whether it be that *small things make mean men proud*,[2] and vanity catches small occasions; or that all contrariety of opinion, even in those that can defend it no longer, makes proud men angry; there is often found in

[1] Zachary Grey, 2 vols., 1754. (See Sherbo, pp. 41–42, 52.)
[2] *2 Henry VI*, IV. i. 106: "Small things make base men proud."

commentators a spontaneous strain of invective and contempt, more eager and venomous than is vented by the most furious controvertist in politics against those whom he is hired to defame.

Perhaps the lightness of the matter may conduce to the vehemence of the agency; when the truth to be investigated is so near to inexistence as to escape attention, its bulk is to be enlarged by rage and exclamation. That to which all would be indifferent in its original state may attract notice when the fate of a name is appended to it. A commentator has indeed great temptations to supply by turbulence what he wants of dignity, to beat his little gold to a spacious surface, to work that to foam which no art or diligence can exalt to spirit.

The notes which I have borrowed or written are either illustrative, by which difficulties are explained; or judicial, by which faults and beauties are remarked; or emendatory, by which depravations are corrected.

The explanations transcribed from others, if I do not subjoin any other interpretation, I suppose commonly to be right, at least I intend by acquiescence to confess that I have nothing better to propose.

After the labors of all the editors, I found many passages which appeared to me likely to obstruct the greater number of readers and thought it my duty to facilitate their passage. It is impossible for an expositor not to write too little for some and too much for others. He can only judge what is necessary by his own experience; and, how long soever he may deliberate, will at last explain many lines which the learned will think impossible to be mistaken and omit many for which the ignorant will want his help. These are censures merely relative and must be quietly endured. I have endeavored to be neither superfluously copious nor scrupulously reserved, and hope that I have made my author's meaning accessible to many who before were frighted from perusing him, and contributed something to the public, by diffusing innocent and rational pleasure.

The complete explanation of an author not systematic and consequential but desultory and vagrant, abounding in casual allusions and light hints, is not to be expected from any single scholiast. All personal reflections, when names are suppressed, must be in a few years irrecover-

ably obliterated; and customs too minute to attract the
notice of law, such as modes of dress, formalities of conversation, rules of visits, disposition of furniture, and practices of ceremony, which naturally find places in familiar
dialogue, are so fugitive and unsubstantial that they are
not easily retained or recovered. What can be known will
be collected by chance from the recesses of obscure and
obsolete papers perused commonly with some other view.
Of this knowledge every man has some, and none has
much; but when an author has engaged the public attention, those who can add anything to his illustration communicate their discoveries, and time produces what had
eluded diligence.

To time I have been obliged to resign many passages
which, though I did not understand them, will perhaps
hereafter be explained; having, I hope, illustrated some
which others have neglected or mistaken, sometimes by
short remarks or marginal directions, such as every editor
has added at his will, and often by comments more laborious than the matter will seem to deserve; but that which
is most difficult is not always most important, and to an
editor nothing is a trifle by which his author is obscured.

The poetical beauties or defects I have not been very
diligent to observe. Some plays have more and some fewer
judicial observations, not in proportion to their difference
of merit, but because I gave this part of my design to
chance and to caprice. The reader, I believe, is seldom
pleased to find his opinion anticipated; it is natural to delight more in what we find or make than in what we receive. Judgment, like other faculties, is improved by practice, and its advancement is hindered by submission to
dictatorial decisions, as the memory grows torpid by the
use of a table-book. Some initiation is, however, necessary.
Of all skill, part is infused by precept, and part is obtained by habit; I have therefore shown so much as may
enable the candidate of criticism to discover the rest.

To the end of most plays I have added short strictures,
containing a general censure of faults or praise of excellence; in which I know not how much I have concurred
with the current opinion; but I have not, by any affectation of singularity, deviated from it. Nothing is minutely
and particularly examined, and therefore it is to be supposed that in the plays which are condemned there is

much to be praised, and in those which are praised much to be condemned.

The part of criticism in which the whole succession of editors has labored with the greatest diligence, which has occasioned the most arrogant ostentation and excited the keenest acrimony, is the emendation of corrupted passages, to which the public attention, having been first drawn by the violence of contention between Pope and Theobald, has been continued by the persecution which, with a kind of conspiracy, has been since raised against all the publishers of Shakespeare.

That many passages have passed in a state of depravation through all the editions is indubitably certain; of these the restoration is only to be attempted by collation of copies or sagacity of conjecture. The collator's province is safe and easy, the conjecturer's perilous and difficult. Yet as the greater part of the plays are extant only in one copy, the peril must not be avoided nor the difficulty refused.

Of the readings which this emulation of amendment has hitherto produced, some from the labors of every publisher I have advanced into the text; those are to be considered as in my opinion sufficiently supported; some I have rejected without mention, as evidently erroneous; some I have left in the notes without censure or approbation, as resting in equipoise between objection and defense; and some, which seemed specious but not right, I have inserted with a subsequent animadversion.

Having classed the observations of others, I was at last to try what I could substitute for their mistakes and how I could supply their omissions. I collated such copies as I could procure and wished for more, but have not found the collectors of these rarities very communicative. Of the editions which chance or kindness put into my hands I have given an enumeration, that I may not be blamed for neglecting what I had not the power to do.

By examining the old copies, I soon found that the later publishers, with all their boasts of diligence, suffered many passages to stand unauthorized, and contented themselves with Rowe's regulation of the text even where they knew it to be arbitrary and with a little consideration might have found it to be wrong. Some of these alterations are only the ejection of a word for one that appeared to him more elegant or more intelligible. These corruptions I have often silently rectified; for the history of our language and the true force of our words can only be preserved by keeping the text of authors free from adulteration. Others, and those very frequent, smoothed the cadence or regulated the measure; on these I have not exercised the same rigor; if only a word was transposed or a particle inserted or omitted, I have sometimes suffered the line to stand; for the inconstancy of the copies is such as that some liberties may be easily permitted. But this practice I have not suffered to proceed far, having restored the primitive diction wherever it could for any reason be preferred.

The emendations which comparison of copies supplied I have inserted in the text; sometimes, where the improvement was slight, without notice, and sometimes with an account of the reasons of the change.

Conjecture, though it be sometimes unavoidable, I have not wantonly nor licentiously indulged. It has been my settled principle that the reading of the ancient books is probably true and therefore is not to be disturbed for the sake of elegance, perspicuity, or mere improvement of the sense. For though much credit is not due to the fidelity, nor any to the judgment, of the first publishers, yet they who had the copy before their eyes were more likely to read it right than we who read it only by imagination. But it is evident that they have often made strange mistakes by ignorance or negligence, and that therefore something may be properly attempted by criticism, keeping the middle way between presumption and timidity.

Such criticism I have attempted to practice, and, where any passage appeared inextricably perplexed, have endeavored to discover how it may be recalled to sense with least violence. But my first labor is always to turn the old text on every side and try if there be any interstice through which light can find its way; nor would Huetius [1] himself condemn me as refusing the trouble of research for the ambition of alteration. In this modest industry I have not been unsuccessful. I have rescued many lines from the violations of temerity and secured many scenes from the inroads of correction. I have adopted the Roman sentiment, that it is more honorable to save a citizen than to kill an enemy, and have been more careful to protect than to attack.

[1] Pierre Huet, *De Interpretatione*, 1661.

I have preserved the common distribution of the plays into acts, though I believe it to be in almost all the plays void of authority. Some of those which are divided in the later editions have no division in the first folio, and some that are divided in the folio have no division in the preceding copies. The settled mode of the theater requires four intervals in the play; but few, if any, of our author's compositions can be properly distributed in that manner. An act is so much of the drama as passes without intervention of time or change of place. A pause makes a new act. In every real, and therefore in every imitative action, the intervals may be more or fewer, the restriction of five acts being accidental and arbitrary. This Shakespeare knew, and this he practiced; his plays were written and at first printed in one unbroken continuity and ought now to be exhibited with short pauses interposed as often as the scene is changed or any considerable time is required to pass. This method would at once quell a thousand absurdities.

In restoring the author's works to their integrity, I have considered the punctuation as wholly in my power; for what could be their care of colons and commas who corrupted words and sentences? Whatever could be done by adjusting points is therefore silently performed, in some plays with much diligence, in others with less; it is hard to keep a busy eye steadily fixed upon evanescent atoms or a discursive mind upon evanescent truth.

The same liberty has been taken with a few particles or other words of slight effect. I have sometimes inserted or omitted them without notice. I have done that sometimes which the other editors have done always, and which indeed the state of the text may sufficiently justify.

The greater part of readers, instead of blaming us for passing trifles, will wonder that on mere trifles so much labor is expended, with such importance of debate, and such solemnity of diction. To these I answer with confidence that they are judging of an art which they do not understand; yet cannot much reproach them with their ignorance nor promise that they would become in general, by learning criticism, more useful, happier, or wiser.

As I practiced conjecture more, I learned to trust it less; and after I had printed a few plays, resolved to insert none of my own readings in the text. Upon this caution I now congratulate myself, for every day increases my doubt of my emendations.

Since I have confined my imagination to the margin, it must not be considered as very reprehensible if I have suffered it to play some freaks in its own dominion. There is no danger in conjecture if it be proposed as conjecture; and while the text remains uninjured, those changes may be safely offered which are not considered even by him that offers them as necessary or safe.

If my readings are of little value, they have not been ostentatiously displayed or importunately obtruded. I could have written longer notes, for the art of writing notes is not of difficult attainment. The work is performed, first by railing at the stupidity, negligence, ignorance, and asinine tastelessness of the former editors, and showing, from all that goes before and all that follows, the inelegance and absurdity of the old reading; then by proposing something which to superficial readers would seem specious, but which the editor rejects with indignation; then by producing the true reading, with a long paraphrase, and concluding with loud acclamations on the discovery and a sober wish for the advancement and prosperity of genuine criticism.

All this may be done, and perhaps done sometimes without impropriety. But I have always suspected that the reading is right which requires many words to prove it wrong; and the emendation wrong that cannot without so much labor appear to be right. The justness of a happy restoration strikes at once, and the moral precept may be well applied to criticism, *quod dubitas ne feceris*.[1]

To dread the shore which he sees spread with wrecks is natural to the sailor. I had before my eye so many critical adventures ended in miscarriage that caution was forced upon me. I encountered in every page Wit struggling with its own sophistry, and Learning confused by the multiplicity of its views. I was forced to censure those whom I admired and could not but reflect, while I was dispossessing their emendations, how soon the same fate might happen to my own, and how many of the readings which I have corrected may be by some other editor defended or established.

---

[1] When in doubt, don't do it.

> Critics I saw, that others' names efface,
> And fix their own with labor in the place;
> Their own, like others, soon their place resign'd,
> Or disappear'd and left the first behind.   Pope.[1]

That a conjectural critic should often be mistaken, cannot be wonderful, either to others or himself, if it be considered that in his art there is no system, no principal and axiomatical truth that regulates subordinate positions. His chance of error is renewed at every attempt; an oblique view of the passage, a slight misapprehension of a phrase, a casual inattention to the parts connected, is sufficient to make him not only fail, but fail ridiculously; and when he succeeds best, he produces perhaps but one reading of many probable, and he that suggests another will always be able to dispute his claims.

It is an unhappy state in which danger is hid under pleasure. The allurements of emendation are scarcely resistible. Conjecture has all the joy and all the pride of invention, and he that has once started a happy change is too much delighted to consider what objections may rise against it.

Yet conjectural criticism has been of great use in the learned world; nor is it my intention to depreciate a study that has exercised so many mighty minds, from the revival of learning to our own age, from the bishop of Aleria [2] to English Bentley.[3] The critics on ancient authors have, in the exercise of their sagacity, many assistances which the editor of Shakespeare is condemned to want. They are employed upon grammatical and settled languages, whose construction contributes so much to perspicuity that Homer has fewer passages unintelligible than Chaucer. The words have not only a known regimen but invariable quantities, which direct and confine the choice. There are commonly more manuscripts than one; and they do not often conspire in the same mistakes. Yet Scaliger could confess to Salmasius how little satisfaction his emendations gave him. *Illudunt nobis conjecturae nostrae, quarum nos pudet, posteaquam in meliores codices in-*

---

[1] *Temple of Fame,* ll. 37–40, with slight variations.

[2] Joannes Andreas (1417–c.1480) was librarian to Pope Sixtus IV.

[3] Richard Bentley (1662–1742), Keeper of the King's Libraries, Master of Trinity College, Cambridge, famous for his emendations of the texts of Horace and Manilius.

cidimus.[1] And Lipsius could complain that critics were making faults by trying to remove them, *Ut olim vitiis, ita nunc remediis laboratur.*[2] And indeed, where mere conjecture is to be used, the emendations of Scaliger and Lipsius, notwithstanding their wonderful sagacity and erudition, are often vague and disputable, like mine or Theobald's.

Perhaps I may not be more censured for doing wrong than for doing little; for raising in the public expectations which at last I have not answered. The expectation of ignorance is indefinite, and that of knowledge is often tyrannical. It is hard to satisfy those who know not what to demand, or those who demand by design what they think impossible to be done. I have indeed disappointed no opinion more than my own; yet I have endeavored to perform my task with no slight solicitude. Not a single passage in the whole work has appeared to me corrupt which I have not attempted to restore; or obscure which I have not endeavored to illustrate. In many I have failed, like others; and from many, after all my efforts, I have retreated and confessed the repulse. I have not passed over, with affected superiority, what is equally difficult to the reader and to myself, but, where I could not instruct him, have owned my ignorance. I might easily have accumulated a mass of seeming learning upon easy scenes; but it ought not to be imputed to negligence that, where nothing was necessary, nothing has been done, or that, where others have said enough, I have said no more.

Notes are often necessary, but they are necessary evils. Let him that is yet unacquainted with the powers of Shakespeare and who desires to feel the highest pleasure that the drama can give, read every play, from the first scene to the last, with utter negligence of all his commenta-

[1] "Our conjectures make us look silly; we are ashamed of them after we have come upon better manuscripts." Joseph Justus Scaliger (1540–1609), French philologist, was the "founder of historical criticism." The quotation is from a letter of July 1608 to Claude de Saumaise (1583–1653), to be found in Scaliger's *Opuscula Varia antehac Non Edita* (Paris, 1610), p. 469.

[2] The Latin is paraphrased in the preceding words of Johnson. Justus Lipsius (1547–1606), Flemish humanist, professor at Jena and later at Leyden, was succeeded at Leyden by Scaliger. See his *Ad Annales Cornelii Taciti Liber Commentarius sive Notae* (Antwerp, 1581), *Ad Lectorem,* signature *5, line 19.

tors. When his fancy is once on the wing, let it not stoop at correction or explanation. When his attention is strongly engaged, let it disdain alike to turn aside to the name of Theobald and of Pope. Let him read on through brightness and obscurity, through integrity and corruption; let him preserve his comprehension of the dialogue and his interest in the fable. And when the pleasures of novelty have ceased, let him attempt exactness and read the commentators.

Particular passages are cleared by notes, but the general effect of the work is weakened. The mind is refrigerated by interruption; the thoughts are diverted from the principal subject; the reader is weary, he suspects not why, and at last throws away the book which he has too diligently studied.

Parts are not to be examined till the whole has been surveyed; there is a kind of intellectual remoteness necessary for the comprehension of any great work in its full design and in its true proportions; a close approach shows the smaller niceties, but the beauty of the whole is discerned no longer.

It is not very grateful to consider how little the succession of editors has added to this author's power of pleasing. He was read, admired, studied, and imitated, while he was yet deformed with all the improprieties which ignorance and neglect could accumulate upon him; while the reading was yet not rectified nor his allusions understood; yet then did Dryden pronounce that "Shakespeare was the man who of all modern and perhaps ancient poets had the largest and most comprehensive soul."

All the images of nature were still present to him, and he drew them not laboriously but luckily; when he describes anything, you more than see it, you feel it too. Those who accuse him to have wanted learning give him the greater commendation; he was naturally learned; he needed not the spectacles of books to read nature; he looked inwards and found her there. I cannot say he is everywhere alike; were he so, I should do him injury to compare him with the greatest of mankind. He is many times flat and insipid; his comic wit degenerating into clenches, his serious swelling into bombast. But he is always great when some great occasion is presented to him; no man can say he ever had a fit subject for his wit and did not then raise himself as high above the rest of poets

Quantum lenta solent inter viburna cupressi.[1]

It is to be lamented that such a writer should want a commentary; that his language should become obsolete or his sentiments obscure. But it is vain to carry wishes beyond the condition of human things; that which must happen to all, has happened to Shakespeare, by accident and time; and more than has been suffered by any other writer since the use of types has been suffered by him through his own negligence of fame or perhaps by that superiority of mind which despised its own performances when it compared them with its powers, and judged those works unworthy to be preserved which the critics of following ages were to contend for the fame of restoring and explaining.

Among these candidates of inferior fame, I am now to stand the judgment of the public; and wish that I could confidently produce my commentary as equal to the encouragement which I have had the honor of receiving. Every work of this kind is by its nature deficient, and I should feel little solicitude about the sentence were it to be pronounced only by the skillful and the learned.

[1] Dryden, *An Essay of Dramatic Poesy*, 1668 (*Essays*, ed. W. P. Ker, 1926, I. 79–80); Virgil, *Eclogues*, I. 25: ". . . as cypresses do among the bending osiers."

NOTES [1765]

From Johnson's edition of
The Plays of William Shakespeare, 1765

The text follows that of 1765, with a few later additions, which are indicated. (Johnson reprinted his 1745 *Observations on Macbeth* in 1765 almost verbatim. My text of the *Macbeth* notes follows 1765, but passages *added* to the text of 1745 are indicated.)

The notes are grouped by plays—comedies, histories, tragedies—in the order of Johnson's edition of 1765.

The short quotations from Shakespeare's text or the stage directions by which Johnson in 1765 cued his notes have been in some instances expanded (as by Steevens in 1773, or even further); the spelling and punctuation of these have been modernized according to W. J. Craig's Oxford text of 1930, as with Shakespeare quotations throughout this volume; but the words of the Shakespeare text have been left as Johnson read them.

A few of the notes have been included mainly for the sake of illustrating some general characteristic of Johnson's editorial mind: for instance, his half-suspicious awareness of verbal ambiguities, or the kinds of historical knowledge which he put to good use. But the selection includes mainly longer notes, or groups of shorter notes, which have a substantial critical bearing on specific plays. A few supplementary passages from Johnson's biographers are inserted at appropriate places.

G. W. Stone, *PMLA*, March 1950, has adduced a wealth of illustration to show how the realistic and emotive acting of Garrick, replacing the traditional declamatory style, had by 1765 already promoted a shift in popular criticism, from the neoclassic censure of plots and marking of beauties and faults, to a chorus of interest in Shakespeare's character portrayal. D. N. Smith, 1928, pp. 79ff., points out that, whereas Johnson's Preface is the climax of the older tradition of general Shakespeare celebration, the Notes to his edition exhibit a detailed concern with Shakespeare's characters which heralds the new school of Shakespearian character study—William Richardson (1774), Maurice Morgann (1777), Thomas Whately

(1785), Richard Cumberland and Henry Mackenzie (1786). "Character" was to be the main vogue in Shakespeare criticism until its ultimate development at the end of the nineteenth century in the work of A. C. Bradley.

The Tempest

I. ii. 250. *Prospero*. Dost thou forget / From what a torment I did free thee?] That the character and conduct of Prospero may be understood, something must be known of the system of enchantment which supplied all the marvelous found in the romances of the Middle Ages. This system seems to be founded on the opinion that the fallen spirits, having different degrees of guilt, had different habitations allotted them at their expulsion, some being confined in hell, *some* (as Hooker, who delivers the opinion of our poet's age, expresses it) *dispersed in air, some on earth, some in water, others in caves, dens, or minerals under the earth.* Of these, some were more malignant and mischievous than others. The earthy spirits seem to have been thought the most depraved, and the aerial the least vitiated. Thus Prospero observes of Ariel:

> Thou wast a spirit too delicate
> To act her *earthy* and abhorr'd commands.

Over these spirits a power might be obtained by certain rites performed or charms learned. This power was called *The Black Art* or *Knowledge of Enchantment.* The enchanter being, as King James observes in his *Demonology*, one *who commands the devil, whereas the witch serves him.* Those who thought best of this art, the existence of which was, I am afraid, believed very seriously, held that certain sounds and characters had a physical power over spirits and compelled their agency; others who condemned the practice, which in reality was surely never practiced, were of opinion, with more reason, that the power of charms arose *only* from compact and was no more than the spirits voluntar[il]y allowed them for the seduction of man. The art was held by all, though not equally criminal, yet unlawful, and therefore Causabon, speaking of one who had commerce with spirits, blames him, though he

imagines him *one of the best kind who dealt with them by
way of command*. Thus Prospero repents of his art in the
last scene. The spirits were always considered as in some
measure enslaved to the enchanter, at least for a time, and
as serving with unwillingness; therefore Ariel so often
begs for liberty; and Caliban observes that the spirits serve
Prospero with no good will but *hate him rootedly*.—Of
these trifles enough.

I. ii. 321. *Caliban*.

> As wicked dew, as e'er my mother brush'd
> With raven's feather from unwholesome fen,
> Drop on you both!]

Whence these critics [Bentley and others] derived the notion of a new language appropriated to Caliban, I cannot
find; they certainly mistook brutality of sentiment for un-
couthness of words. Caliban had learned to speak of
Prospero and his daughter, he had no names for the sun
and the moon before their arrival, and could not have invented a language of his own without more understanding than Shakespeare has thought it proper to bestow
upon him. His diction is indeed somewhat clouded by the
gloominess of his temper and the malignity of his purposes;
but let any other being entertain the same thoughts, and
he will find them easily issue in the same expressions.

General Observation. It is observed of *The Tempest* that
its plan is regular; this the author of the *Revisal* thinks,
what I think too, an accidental effect of the story, not intended or regarded by our author. But whatever might
be Shakespeare's intention in forming or adapting the plot,
he has made it instrumental to the production of many
characters, diversified with boundless invention, and preserved with profound skill in nature, extensive knowledge
of opinions, and accurate observation of life. In a single
drama are here exhibited princes, courtiers, and sailors, all
speaking in their real characters. There is the agency of
airy spirits and of an earthly goblin. The operation of
magic, the tumults of a storm, the adventures of a desert
island, the native effusion of untaught affection, the punishment of guilt, and the final happiness of the pair for
whom our passions and reason are equally interested.[1]

[1] This note is added in 1773.

A Midsummer Night's Dream

I. ii. *Enter* Quince *the carpenter,* Snug *the joiner,* Bottom *the weaver,* Flute *the bellows-mender,* Snout *the tinker, and* Starveling *the tailor.*] In this scene Shakespeare takes advantage of his knowledge of the theater to ridicule the prejudices and competitions of the players. Bottom, who is generally acknowledged the principal actor, declares his inclination to be for a tyrant, for a part of fury, tumult, and noise, such as every young man pants to perform when he first steps upon the stage. The same Bottom, who seems bred in a tiring room, has another histrionical passion. He is for engrossing every part and would exclude his inferiors from all possibility of distinction. He is therefore desirous to play Pyramus, Thisbe, and the Lion at the same time.

I. ii. 50. *Flute.* Nay, faith, let not me play a woman; I have a beard coming. *Quince.* That's all one: you shall play it in a mask; and you may speak as small as you will.] This passage shows how the want of women on the old stage was supplied. If they had not a young man who could perform the part with a face that might pass for feminine, the character was acted in a mask, which was at that time part of a lady's dress so much in use that it did not [1] give any unusual appearance to the scene; and he that could modulate his voice in a female tone might play the woman very successfully. It is observed in Downes's *Memoirs of the Playhouse* that one of these counterfeit heroines moved the passions more strongly than the women that have since been brought upon the stage. Some of the catastrophes of the old comedies, which make lovers marry the wrong women, are, by recollection of the common use of masks, brought nearer to probability.

III. i. In the time of Shakespeare, there were many companies of players, sometimes five at the same time, contending for the favor of the public. Of these some were undoubtedly very unskillful and very poor, and it is

[1] 1765 omits "not"; it is added in 1773.

probable that the design of this scene was to ridicule their
ignorance and the odd expedients to which they might be
driven by the want of proper decorations. Bottom was perhaps the head of a rival house and is therefore honored
with an ass's head.

V. i. 148. *Prologue. Whereat, with blade, with bloody
blameful blade*] Mr. Upton rightly observes that Shakespeare in this line ridicules the affectation of beginning
many words with the same letter. He might have remarked
the same of

> The raging rocks
> And shivering shocks.

Gascoigne, contemporary with our poet, remarks and
blames the same affectation.

General Observation. Of this play there are two editions
in the quarto, one printed for Thomas Fisher, the other for
James Roberts, both in 1600. I have used the copy of
Roberts, very carefully collated, as it seems, with that of
Fisher. Neither of the editions approach to exactness.
Fisher is sometimes preferable, but Roberts was followed,
though not without some variations, by Heming and
Condell, and they by all the folios that succeeded them.

Wild and fantastical as this play is, all the parts in their
various modes are well written and give the kind of pleasure which the author designed. Fairies in his time were
much in fashion; common tradition had made them familiar, and Spenser's poem had made them great.[1]

Measure for Measure

There is perhaps not one of Shakespeare's plays more
darkened than this by the peculiarities of its author and
the unskillfulness of its editors, by distortions of phrase
or negligence of transcription.

III. i. 14. *Duke.* For all th' accommodations, that thou
bear'st / Are nurs'd by baseness.] Dr. Warburton is undoubtedly mistaken in supposing that by *baseness* is meant

[1] The second paragraph of this note follows the edition of
1773.

self-love here assigned as the motive of all human actions. Shakespeare only meant to observe that a minute analysis of life at once destroys that splendor which dazzles the imagination. Whatever grandeur can display or luxury enjoy is procured by *baseness,* by offices of which the mind shrinks from the contemplation. All the delicacies of the table may be traced back to the shambles and the dung-hill, all magnificence of building was hewn from the quarry, and all the pomp of ornaments dug from among the damps and darkness of the mine.

III. i. 17. *Duke.*

> Thy best of rest is sleep,
> And that thou oft provok'st; yet grossly fear'st
> Thy death, which is no more.]

Here Dr. Warburton might have found a sentiment worthy of his animadversion. I cannot without indignation find Shakespeare saying that *death is only sleep,* lengthening out his exhortation by a sentence which in the friar is impious, in the reasoner is foolish, and in the poet trite and vulgar.

III. i. 32. *Duke.*

> Thou hast nor youth nor age;
> But, as it were, an after-dinner's sleep,
> Dreaming on both.]

This is exquisitely imagined. When we are young, we busy ourselves in forming schemes for succeeding time and miss the gratifications that are before us; when we are old, we amuse the languor of age with the recollection of youthful pleasures or performances; so that our life, of which no part is filled with the business of the present time, resembles our dreams after dinner, when the events of the morning are mingled with the designs of the evening.

III. i. 111. *Claudio.*

> If it were damnable, he being so wise,
> Why would he for the momentary trick
> Be perdurably fin'd?]

Shakespeare shows his knowledge of human nature in the conduct of Claudio. When Isabella first tells him of Angelo's proposal, he answers, with honest indignation, agreeably to his settled principles,

> Thou shalt not do't.

But the love of life, being permitted to operate, soon furnishes him with sophistical arguments; he believes it cannot be very dangerous to the soul, since Angelo, who is so wise, will venture it.

III. i. 137. *Isabella.* Is't not a kind of incest, to take life / From thine own sister's shame?] In Isabella's declamation there is something harsh and something forced and far-fetched. But her indignation cannot be thought violent when we consider her not only as a virgin but as a nun.

V. i. 448. *Isabella.* Till he did look on me] The duke has justly observed that Isabel is *importuned against all sense* to solicit for Angelo, yet here *against all sense* she solicits for him. Her argument is extraordinary.

> A due sincerity govern'd his deeds,
> Till he did look on me: since it is so,
> Let him not die.

That Angelo had committed all the crimes charged against him, as far as he could commit them, is evident. The only *intent* which *his* act did not overtake was the defilement of Isabel. Of this Angelo was only intentionally guilty.

Angelo's crimes were such as must sufficiently justify punishment, whether its end be to secure the innocent from wrong or to deter guilt by example; and I believe every reader feels some indignation when he finds him spared. From what extenuation of his crime can Isabel, who yet supposes her brother dead, form any plea in his favor. *Since he was good, 'till he looked on me, let him not die.* I am afraid our varlet poet intended to inculcate that women think ill of nothing that raises the credit of their beauty and are ready, however virtuous, to pardon any act which they think incited by their own charms.

V. i. 495. *Duke.* By this, Lord Angelo perceives he's safe.] It is somewhat strange that Isabel is not made to express either gratitude, wonder, or joy at the sight of her brother.

V. i. 500. *Duke.* And yet here's one in place I cannot pardon.] After the pardon of two murderers, Lucio might be

treated by the good duke with less harshness; but perhaps
the poet intended to show, what is too often seen, *that
men easily forgive wrongs which are not committed
against themselves.*

As You Like It

I. i. 60. *Orlando.* I am no villain.] The word *villain* is used
by the elder brother, in its present meaning, for a *worth-
less, wicked,* or *bloody man;* by Orlando in its original sig-
nification, for a *fellow of base extraction.*

I. iii. 33. *Celia.* you should love his son dearly? By this
kind of chase, I should hate him, for my father hated his
father dearly.] That is, by this way of *following* the argument. *Dear* is used by Shakespeare in a double sense, for
beloved, and for *hurtful, hated, baleful.* Both senses are
authorized, and both drawn from etymology, but properly
beloved is *dear,* and *hateful* is *dere.* Rosalind uses *dearly*
in the good, and Celia in the bad sense.

II. i. 13. *Duke.*

> Which like the toad, ugly and venomous,
> Wears yet a precious jewel in his head]

It was the current opinion in Shakespeare's time that in
the head of an old toad was to be found a stone, or pearl,
to which great virtues were ascribed. This stone has been
often sought, but nothing has been found more than accidental or perhaps morbid indurations of the skull.

III. iv. 10. *Rosalind.* I' faith, his hair is of a good colour.]
There is much of nature in this petty perverseness of Rosalind; she finds faults in her lover, in hope to be contra-
dicted, and when Celia in sportive malice too readily sec-
onds her accusations, she contradicts herself rather than
suffer her favorite to want a vindication.

IV. i. 40. *Rosalind.* swam in a gondola] That is, *been at*
Venice, the seat at that time of all licentiousness, where
the young English gentlemen wasted their fortunes, debased their morals, and sometimes lost their religion.
The fashion of traveling, which prevailed very much in

our author's time, was considered by the wiser men as one of the principal causes of corrupt manners. It was therefore gravely censured by Ascham in his *Schoolmaster* and by Bishop Hall in his *Quo Vadis;* and is here, and in other passages, ridiculed by Shakespeare.

General Observation. Of this play the fable is wild and pleasing. I know not how the ladies will approve the facility with which both Rosalind and Celia give away their hearts. To Celia much may be forgiven for the heroism of her friendship. The character of Jaques is natural and well preserved. The comic dialogue is very sprightly, with less mixture of low buffoonery than in some other plays; and the graver part is elegant and harmonious. By hastening to the end of his work, Shakespeare suppressed the dialogue between the usurper and the hermit and lost an opportunity of exhibiting a moral lesson in which he might have found matter worthy of his highest powers.

Love's Labour's Lost

IV. ii. *Enter* Holofernes, Sir Nathaniel, *and* Dull.] I am not of the learned commentator's [Warburton's] opinion that the satire of Shakespeare is so seldom personal. It is of the nature of personal invectives to be soon unintelligible; and the author that gratifies private malice *animam in vulnere ponit,* destroys the future efficacy of his own writings and sacrifices the esteem of succeeding times to the laughter of a day. It is no wonder, therefore, that the sarcasms which, perhaps in the author's time, set the playhouse in a roar, are now lost among general reflections. Yet whether the character of Holofernes was pointed at any particular man, I am, notwithstanding the plausibility of Dr. Warburton's conjecture, inclined to doubt. Every man adheres as long as he can to his own preconceptions. Before I read this note I considered the character of Holofernes as borrowed from the Rhombus of Sir Philip Sidney, who, in a kind of pastoral entertainment exhibited to Queen Elizabeth, has introduced a schoolmaster so called, speaking *a leash of languages at once* and puzzling himself and his auditors with a jargon like that of Holofernes in the present play. Sidney himself might bring the character from Italy; for, as Peacham observes, the schoolmaster has long been one of the ridiculous personages in the farces of that country. [Warburton had conjectured that Holofernes represented the Italian scholar John Florio. Sidney's pastoral entertainment was *The Lady of the May*, 1578.]

V. i. 2. *Sir Nathaniel.* your reasons at dinner have been sharp and sententious.] I know not well what degree of respect Shakespeare intends to obtain for this vicar, but he has here put into his mouth a finished representation of colloquial excellence. It is very difficult to add any thing to this character of the schoolmaster's table-talk, and perhaps all the precepts of Castiglione will scarcely be found to comprehend a rule for conversation so justly delineated, so widely dilated, and so nicely limited. . . .

V. ii. 789. *Princess.* As bombast and as lining to the time] This line is obscure. *Bombast* was a kind of loose texture not unlike what is now called wadding, used to give the dresses of that time bulk and protuberance, without much increase of weight; whence the same name is yet given a tumor of words unsupported by solid sentiment. The princess, therefore, says, that they considered this courtship as but *bombast,* as something to fill out life, which not being closely united with it, might be thrown away at pleasure.

General Observation. In this play, which all the editors have concurred to censure and some have rejected as unworthy of our poet, it must be confessed that there are many passages mean, childish, and vulgar; and some which ought not to have been exhibited, as we are told they were, to a maiden queen. But there are scattered through the whole many sparks of genius; nor is there any play that has more evident marks of the hand of Shakespeare.

The Winter's Tale

III. i. 2. *Cleomenes.* Fertile the isle] [Warburton had argued that "isle" is incorrect geographically and had suggested "soil."] Shakespeare is little careful of geography.

There is no need of this emendation in a play in which the whole plot depends upon a geographical error, by which Bohemia is supposed to be a maritime country.

III. ii. 173. *Leontes.* Does my deeds make the blacker!] This vehement retraction of Leontes, accompanied with the confession of more crimes than he was suspected of, is agreeable to our daily experience of the vicissitudes of violent tempers and the eruptions of minds oppressed with guilt.

General Observation. Of this play no edition is known published before the folio of 1623.

The story is taken from the novel of *Dorastus and Faunia,* which may be read in *Shakespeare Illustrated.*

This play, as Dr. Warburton justly observes, is, with all its absurdities, very entertaining. The character of Autolycus is very naturally conceived and strongly represented.

Twelfth Night

II. v. 67. *Malvolio.* wind up my watch] In our author's time watches were very uncommon. When Guy Fawkes was taken, it was urged as a circumstance of suspicion that a watch was found upon him.

III. iv. 260. *Sir Toby Belch.* He is knight dubb'd with unhack'd rapier, and on carpet consideration.] That is, he is no soldier by profession, not a Knight Banneret, dubbed in the field of battle, but, *on carpet consideration,* at a festivity, or on some peaceable occasion, when knights receive their dignity kneeling not on the ground, as in war, but on a carpet. This is, I believe, the original of the contemptuous term a *carpet knight,* who was naturally held in scorn by the men of war.

IV. ii. 134. *Clown.* like to the old Vice] *Vice* was the fool of the old moralities. Some traces of this character are still preserved in puppet shows and by country mummers.

General Observation. This play is in the graver part elegant and easy, and in some of the lighter scenes exquisitely humorous. Aguecheek is drawn with great propriety, but his character is, in a great measure, that of natural fatuity and is therefore not the proper prey of a satirist. The soliloquy of Malvolio is truly comic; he is betrayed to ridicule merely by his pride. The marriage of Olivia and the succeeding perplexity, though well enough contrived to divert on the stage, wants credibility and fails to produce the proper instruction required in the drama, as it exhibits no just picture of life.

The Merry Wives of Windsor

III. i. 157. *Ford.* I'll be horn-mad.] There is no image which our author appears so fond of as that of a cuckold's horns. Scarcely a light character is introduced that does not endeavor to produce merriment by some allusion to horned husbands. As he wrote his plays for the stage rather than the press, he perhaps reviewed them seldom and did not observe this repetition, or, finding the jest, however frequent, still successful, did not think correction necessary.

General Observation. Of this play there is a tradition preserved by Mr. Rowe that it was written at the command of Queen Elizabeth, who was so delighted with the character of Falstaff that she wished it to be diffused through more plays; but, suspecting that it might pall by continued uniformity, directed the poet to diversify his manner, by showing him in love. No task is harder than that of writing to the ideas of another. Shakespeare knew what the queen, if the story be true, seems not to have known, that by any real passion of tenderness, the selfish craft, the careless jollity, and the lazy luxury of Falstaff must have suffered so much abatement that little of his former cast would have remained. Falstaff could not love but by ceasing to be Falstaff. He could only counterfeit love, and his professions could be prompted, not by the hope of pleasure, but of money. Thus the poet approached as near as he could to the work enjoined him; yet, having perhaps in the former plays completed his own idea, seems not to have been able to give Falstaff all his former power of entertainment.

This comedy is remarkable for the variety and number of the personages, who exhibit more characters appropriated and discriminated than perhaps can be found in any other play.

Whether Shakespeare was the first that produced upon the English stage the effect of language distorted and depraved by provincial or foreign pronunciations, I cannot certainly decide. This mode of forming ridiculous characters can confer praise only on him who originally discovered it, for it requires not much of either wit or judgment; its success must be derived almost wholly from the player, but its power in a skillful mouth even he that despises it is unable to resist.

The conduct of this drama is deficient; the action begins and ends often before the conclusion, and the different parts might change places without inconvenience; but its general power, that power by which all works of genius shall be finally tried, is such that perhaps it never yet had reader or spectator who did not think it too soon at an end.[1]

The Taming of the Shrew

General Observation. From this play the *Tatler* formed a story, Volume IV, No. 231. [Johnson here presents the *Tatler* story.] It cannot but seem strange that Shakespeare should be so little known to the author of the *Tatler* that he should suffer this story to be obtruded upon him; or so little known to the public that he could hope to make it pass upon his readers as a real narrative of a transaction in Lincolnshire; yet it is apparent that he was deceived or intended to deceive, that he knew not himself whence the story was taken, or hoped that he might rob so obscure a writer without detection.

Of this play the two plots are so well united that they can hardly be called two without injury to the art with which they are interwoven. The attention is entertained with all the variety of a double plot, yet is not distracted by unconnected incidents.

The part between Katharina and Petruchio is eminently spritely and diverting. At the marriage of Bianca the arrival of the real father perhaps produces more perplexity

[1] This note is added in 1773.

than pleasure. The whole play is very popular and diverting.

All's Well That Ends Well

I. iii. *Enter* Countess, Steward, *and* Clown.] A *clown* in Shakespeare is commonly taken for a *licensed jester* or domestic *fool*. We are not to wonder that we find this character often in his plays, since fools were at that time maintained in all great families, to keep up merriment in the house. In the picture of Sir Thomas More's family, by Hans Holbein, the only servant represented is Paterson the *fool*. This is a proof of the familiarity to which they were admitted, not by the great only but the wise.

In some plays, a servant or rustic of remarkable petulance and freedom of speech is likewise called a clown.

IV. ii. 73. *Diana*. Since Frenchmen are so braid, / Marry that will, I'll live and die a maid.] . . . . Nothing is more common than for girls, on such occasions, to say in a pet what they do not think or to think for a time what they do not finally resolve.

V. ii. 58. *Lafeu*. though you are a fool and a knave, you shall eat.] Parolles has many of the lineaments of Falstaff and seems to be the character which Shakespeare delighted to draw, a fellow that had more wit than virtue. Though justice required that he should be detected and exposed, yet his *vices sit so fit in him* that he is not at last suffered to starve.

V. iii. 21. *King*. the first view shall kill / All repetition.] *The first interview shall put an end to all recollection of the past*. Shakespeare is now hastening to the end of the play, finds his matter sufficient to fill up his remaining scenes, and therefore, as on other such occasions, contracts his dialogue and precipitates his action. Decency required that Bertram's double crime of cruelty and disobedience, joined likewise with some hypocrisy, should raise more resentment; and that though his mother might easily forgive him, his king should more pertinaciously vindicate his own authority and Helen's merit. Of all this Shakespeare could not be ignorant, but Shakespeare wanted to conclude his play.

V. iii. 101. *King.* Plutus himself, / That knows the tinct and multiplying medicine] Plutus the grand alchemist, who knows the *tincture* which confers the properties of gold upon base metals, and the *matter* by which *gold* is *multiplied,* by which a small quantity of gold is made to communicate its qualities to a large mass of metal.

In the reign of Henry the Fourth a law was made to forbid *all men thenceforth to* multiply *gold, or use any craft of* multiplication. Of which law Mr. Boyle, when he was warm with the hope of transmutation, procured a repeal.

General Observation. This play has many delightful scenes, though not sufficiently probable, and some happy characters, though not new, nor produced by any deep knowledge of human nature. Parolles is a boaster and a coward, such as has always been the sport of the stage, but perhaps never raised more laughter or contempt than in the hands of Shakespeare.

I cannot reconcile my heart to Bertram; a man noble without generosity, and young without truth; who marries Helen as a coward and leaves her as a profligate; when she is dead by his unkindness, sneaks home to a second marriage, is accused by a woman whom he has wronged, defends himself by falsehood, and is dismissed to happiness.

The story of Bertram and Diana had been told before of Mariana and Angelo, and, to confess the truth, scarcely merited to be heard a second time. The story is copied from a novel of Boccaccio, which may be read in *Shakespeare Illustrated,* with remarks not more favorable to Bertram than my own.

King John

III. i. 70. *Constance.* To me and to the state of my great grief / Let kings assemble.] In *Much Ado about Nothing,* the father of Hero, depressed by her disgrace, declares himself so subdued by grief that *a thread may lead him.*

How is it that grief in Leonato and Lady Constance produces effects directly opposite, and yet both agreeable to nature? Sorrow softens the mind while it is yet warmed by hope, but hardens it when it is congealed by despair. Distress, while there remains any prospect of relief, is weak and flexible, but when no succor remains, is fearless and stubborn; angry alike at those that injure and at those that do not help; careless to please where nothing can be gained, and fearless to offend when there is nothing further to be dreaded. Such was this writer's knowledge of the passions.

IV. ii. 31. *King John.* Hadst thou but shook thy head] There are many touches of nature in this conference of John with Hubert. A man engaged in wickedness would keep the profit to himself and transfer the guilt to his accomplice. These reproaches vented against Hubert are not the words of art or policy, but the eruptions of a mind swelling with consciousness of a crime and desirous of discharging its misery on another.

This account of the timidity of guilt is drawn *ab ipsis recessibus mentis,* from an intimate knowledge of mankind, particularly that line in which he says that *to have bid him tell his tale* in *express* words would have *struck him dumb;* nothing is more certain than that bad men use all the arts of fallacy upon themselves, palliate their actions to their own minds by gentle terms, and hide themselves from their own detection in ambiguities and subterfuges.

General Observation. The tragedy of *King John,* though not written with the utmost power of Shakespeare, is varied with a very pleasing interchange of incidents and characters. The lady's grief is very affecting, and the character of the Bastard contains that mixture of greatness and levity which this author delighted to exhibit.

There is extant another play of *King John,* published with Shakespeare's name, so different from this, and I think from all his other works, that there is reason to think his name was prefixed only to recommend it to sale. No man writes upon the same subject twice without concurring in many places with himself.

King Richard II

I. ii. 53. *Duchess.* A caitiff recreant] *Caitiff* originally signified a *prisoner;* next a *slave,* from the condition of prisoners; then a *scoundrel,* from the qualities of a slave. Ἥμισυ τῆς ἀρετῆς ἀποαίνυται δούλιον ἦμαρ [*Odyssey,* XVII. 322]. In this passage it partakes of all these significations.

III. ii. 93. *King Richard.* Mine ear is open and my heart prepar'd.] It seems to be the design of the poet to raise Richard to esteem in his fall and consequently to interest the reader in his favor. He gives him only passive fortitude, the virtue of a confessor rather than of a king. In his prosperity we saw him imperious and oppressive; but in his distress he is wise, patient, and pious.

III. ii. 207. *King Richard.* I'll hate him everlastingly / That bids me be of comfort any more.] This sentiment is drawn from nature. Nothing is more offensive to a mind convinced that his distress is without a remedy, and preparing to submit quietly to irresistible calamity, than these petty and conjectured comforts which unskillful officiousness thinks it virtue to administer.

III. iii. 156. *King Richard.* where subjects' feet / May hourly trample on their sovereign's head] Shakespeare is very apt to deviate from the pathetic to the ridiculous. Had the speech of Richard ended at this line, it had exhibited the natural language of submissive misery, conforming its intention to the present fortune and calmly ending its purposes in death.

V. iii. 5. *Bolingbroke.*

> Inquire at London, 'mongst the taverns there,
> For there, they say, he daily doth frequent,
> With unrestrained loose companions.]

This is a very proper introduction to the future character of Henry the Fifth, to his debaucheries in his youth and his greatness in his manhood.

General Observation. This play is extracted from the *Chronicle of Holinshed,* in which many passages may be found which Shakespeare has, with very little alteration, transplanted into his scenes; particularly a speech of the bishop of Carlisle in defense of King Richard's unalienable right and immunity from human jurisdiction.

Jonson, who in his *Catiline and Sejanus* has inserted many speeches from the Roman historians, was perhaps induced to that practice by the example of Shakespeare, who had condescended sometimes to copy more ignoble writers. But Shakespeare had more of his own than Jonson and, if he sometimes was willing to spare his labor, showed by what he performed at other times that his extracts were made by choice or idleness rather than necessity.

This play is one of those which Shakespeare has apparently revised; but as success in works of invention is not always proportionate to labor, it is not finished at last with the happy force of some other of his tragedies nor can be said much to affect the passions or enlarge the understanding.

King Henry IV, First Part

I. ii. 233. *Prince Hal*. By so much shall I falsify men's hopes.] . . . This speech is very artfully introduced to keep the prince from appearing vile in the opinion of the audience; it prepares them for his future reformation; and, what is yet more valuable, exhibits a natural picture of a great mind offering excuses to itself and palliating those follies which it can neither justify nor forsake.

I. iii. 201. *Hotspur*.

> By heaven methinks it were an easy leap
> To pluck bright honour from the pale-fac'd moon.]

Though I am far from condemning this speech, with Gildon and Theobald, as absolute madness, yet I cannot find in it that profundity of reflection and beauty of allegory which the learned commentator Warburton has endeavored to display. This sally of Hotspur may be, I think, soberly and rationally vindicated as the violent eruption of a mind inflated with ambition and fired with resentment; as the boasted clamor of a man able to do much and eager to do more; as the hasty motion of turbulent desire; as the

dark expression of indetermined thoughts. The passage
from Euripides [which Warburton adduces] is surely not
allegorical, yet it is produced, and properly, as parallel.

King Henry IV, Second Part

V. v. 70. *King Henry V.* Not to come near our person by
ten mile] Mr. Rowe observes that many readers lament to
see Falstaff so hardly used by his old friend. But if it be
considered that the fat knight has never uttered one sentiment of generosity, and with all his power of exciting
mirth has nothing in him that can be esteemed, no great
pain will be suffered from the reflection that he is compelled to live honestly, and maintained by the king, with
a promise of advancement when he shall deserve it.

I think the poet more blamable for Poins, who is always
represented as joining some virtues with his vices and is
therefore treated by the prince with apparent distinction,
yet he does nothing in the time of action and, though
after the bustle is over he is again a favorite, at last van-
ishes without notice. Shakespeare certainly lost him by
heedlessness, in the multiplicity of his characters, the variety of his action, and his eagerness to end the play.

V. v. 97. *Lord Chief Justice.* Go, carry Sir John Falstaff
to the Fleet.] I do not see why Falstaff is carried to the
Fleet. We have never lost sight of him since his dismission
from the king; he has committed no new fault and therefore incurred no punishment; but the different agitations
of fear, anger, and surprise in him and his company made
a good scene to the eye; and our author, who wanted them
no longer on the stage, was glad to find this method of
sweeping them away.

V. v. 115. *General Observation.* . . . None of Shakespeare's
plays are more read than the *First and Second Parts of
Henry the Fourth.* Perhaps no author has ever in two
plays afforded so much delight. The great events are interesting, for the fate of kingdoms depends upon them; the
slighter occurrences are diverting and, except one or two,
sufficiently probable; the incidents are multiplied with
wonderful fertility of invention, and the characters diversi-

fied with the utmost nicety of discernment and the pro-
foundest skill in the nature of man.

The prince, who is the hero both of the comic and tragic
part, is a young man of great abilities and violent passions,
whose sentiments are right, though his actions are wrong;
whose virtues are obscured by negligence, and whose understanding is dissipated by levity. In his idle hours he is
rather loose than wicked; and when the occasion forces
out his latent qualities, he is great without effort and
brave without tumult. The trifler is roused into a hero, and
the hero again reposes in the trifler. This character is great,
original, and just.

Percy is a rugged soldier, choleric, and quarrelsome,
and has only the soldier's virtues, generosity and courage.

But Falstaff, unimitated, unimitable Falstaff, how shall I
describe thee? Thou compound of sense and vice; of sense
which may be admired but not esteemed, of vice which
may be despised but hardly detested. Falstaff is a character
loaded with faults, and with those faults which naturally
produce contempt. He is a thief and a glutton, a coward
and a boaster, always ready to cheat the weak and prey
upon the poor; to terrify the timorous and insult the de-
fenseless. At once obsequious and malignant, he satirizes
in their absence those whom he lives by flattering. He is
familiar with the prince only as an agent of vice, but of
this familiarity he is so proud as not only to be supercilious
and haughty with common men but to think his interest of
importance to the Duke of Lancaster. Yet the man thus
corrupt, thus despicable, makes himself necessary to the
prince that despises him, by the most pleasing of all qualities, perpetual gaiety, by an unfailing power of exciting
laughter, which is the more freely indulged as his wit is
not of the splendid or ambitious kind but consists in easy
escapes and sallies of levity, which make sport but raise
no envy. It must be observed that he is stained with no
enormous or sanguinary crimes, so that his licentiousness
is not so offensive but that it may be borne for his mirth.

The moral to be drawn from this representation is that
no man is more dangerous than he that, with a will to
corrupt, hath the power to please; and that neither wit
nor honesty ought to think themselves safe with such a
companion when they see Henry seduced by Falstaff.

King Henry V

Prologue. 13. *Chorus*. Within this wooden O] Nothing
shows more evidently the power of custom over language
than that the frequent use of calling a circle an O could so
much hide the meanness of the metaphor from Shakespeare that he has used it many times where he makes his
most eager attempts at dignity of style.

Prologue. 25. *Chorus*. And make imaginary puissance]
This passage shows that Shakespeare was fully sensible of
the absurdity of showing battles on the theater, which indeed is never done but tragedy becomes farce. Nothing
can be represented to the eye but by something like it,
and *within a wooden O* nothing very like a battle can be
exhibited.

II. iii. 27. *Hostess*. cold as any stone] Such is the end of
Falstaff, from whom Shakespeare had promised us in his
epilogue to *Henry IV* that we should receive more
entertainment. It happened to Shakespeare, as to other
writers, to have his imagination crowded with a tumultu-
ary confusion of images which, while they were yet un-
sorted and unexamined, seemed sufficient to furnish a
long train of incidents and a new variety of merriment;
but which, when he was to produce them to view, shrunk
suddenly from him or could not be accommodated to his
general design. That he once designed to have brought
Falstaff on the scene again, we know from himself; but
whether he could contrive no train of adventures suitable
to his character, or could match him with no compan-
ions likely to quicken his humor, or could open no new
vein of pleasantry, and was afraid to continue the same
strain lest it should not find the same reception, he has
here for ever discarded him, perhaps for the same reason
for which Addison killed Sir Roger, that no other hand
might attempt to exhibit him.

Let meaner authors learn from this example that it is
dangerous to sell the bear which is not yet hunted; to promise to the public what they have not written.

This disappointment probably inclined Queen Elizabeth
to command the poet to produce him once again and to

show him in love or courtship. This was indeed a new source of humor and produced a new play from the former characters.

I forgot to note in the proper place, and therefore note here, that Falstaff's courtship, or *The Merry Wives of Windsor,* should be read between *Henry IV* and *Henry V.*

III. iv. *Enter* Katharine, *and an old gentlewoman.*]. ["I have left this ridiculous scene as I found it; and am sorry to have no color left, from any of the editions, to imagine it interpolated." Warburton.] Sir T. Hanmer has rejected it. The scene is indeed mean enough when it is read, but the grimaces of two French women and the odd accent with which they uttered the English made it divert upon the stage. It may be observed that there is in it not only the French language but the French spirit. Alice compliments the princess upon her knowledge of four words and tells her that she pronounces like the English themselves. The princess suspects no deficiency in her instructress, nor the instructress in herself. Throughout the whole scene there may be found French servility and French vanity.

III. vi. 112. *Flute.* his fire's out.] This is the last time that any sport can be made with the red face of Bardolph, which, to confess the truth, seems to have taken more hold on Shakespeare's imagination than on any other. The conception is very cold to the solitary reader, though it may be somewhat invigorated by the exhibition on the stage. This poet is always more careful about the present than the future, about his audience than his readers.

V. i. 92. *Pistol.*

> To England will I steal, and there I'll steal:
> And patches will I get unto these cudgell'd scars,
> And swear I got them in the Gallia wars.]

The comic scenes of *The History of Henry the Fourth* and *Fifth* are now at an end, and all the comic personages are now dismissed. Falstaff and Mrs. Quickly are dead; Nym and Bardolph are hanged; Gadshill was lost immediately after the robbery; Poins and Peto have vanished since, one knows not how; and Pistol is now beaten into obscurity. I believe every reader regrets their departure.

V. ii. 127. *King Henry.* thou wouldst find me such a plain king.] I know not why Shakespeare now gives the king nearly such a character as he made him formerly ridicule in Percy. This military grossness and unskillfulness in all the softer arts does not suit very well with the gaieties of his youth, with the general knowledge ascribed to him at his accession, or with the contemptuous message sent him by the Dauphin, who represents him as fitter for the ball-room than the field and tells him that he is not *to revel into duchies* or win provinces *with a nimble galliard.* The truth is that the poet's matter failed him in the fifth act, and he was glad to fill it up with whatever he could get; and not even Shakespeare can write well without a proper subject. It is a vain endeavor for the most skillful hand to cultivate barrenness or to paint upon vacuity.

General Observation. This play has many scenes of high dignity and many of easy merriment. The character of the king is well supported, except in his courtship, where he has neither the vivacity of Hal nor the grandeur of Henry. The humor of Pistol is very happily continued; his character has perhaps been the model of all the bullies that have yet appeared on the English stage.

The lines given to the Chorus have many admirers; but the truth is that in them a little may be praised and much must be forgiven; nor can it be easily discovered why the intelligence given by the Chorus is more necessary in this play than in many others where it is omitted. The great defect of this play is the emptiness and narrowness of the last act, which a very little diligence might have easily avoided.

[At Versailles the people showed us the theater. As we stood on the stage looking at some machinery for playhouse purposes: "Now we are here, what shall we act, Mr. Johnson, The Englishman at Paris?" "No, no," replied he, "we will try to act Harry the Fifth."—Hester Lynch Thrale Piozzi, *Anecdotes,* in *Johnsonian Miscellanies,* ed. G. B. Hill (Oxford, 1907), I, 216.]

King Richard III

General Observation. This is one of the most celebrated of our author's performances; yet I know not whether it has not happened to him, as to others, to be praised most when praise is not most deserved. That this play has scenes noble in themselves and very well contrived to strike in the exhibition, cannot be denied. But some parts are trifling, others shocking, and some improbable.

King Henry VIII

IV. ii. *Enter* Katharine *Dowager, sick: led between* Griffith *her gentleman-usher and* Patience *her woman.*] This scene is above any other part of Shakespeare's tragedies, and perhaps above any scene of any other poet, tender and pathetic, without gods, or furies, or poisons, or precipices, without the help of romantic circumstances, without improbable sallies of poetical lamentation, and without any throes of tumultuous misery. [See Johnson's note on *Timon of Athens* as a "domestic tragedy" (below p. 99). And for the importance of the "pathetic" in his criticism see Jean H. Hagstrum, *Samuel Johnson's Critical Opinions* (Minneapolis, 1952), pp. 129–152.]

General Observation. The play of *Henry the Eighth* is one of those which still keeps possession of the stage by the splendor of its pageantry. The coronation about forty years ago drew the people together in multitudes for a great part of the winter. Yet pomp is not the only merit of this play. The meek sorrows and virtuous distress of Katharine have furnished some scenes which may be justly numbered among the greatest efforts of tragedy. But the genius of Shakespeare comes in and goes out with Katharine. Every other part may be easily conceived and easily written.

The historical dramas are now concluded, of which the two parts of *Henry the Fourth* and *Henry the Fifth* are among the happiest of our author's compositions; and *King John, Richard the Third,* and *Henry the Eighth* deservedly stand in the second class. Those whose curiosity would refer the historical scenes to their original may consult Holinshed and sometimes Hall; from Holinshed Shakespeare has often inserted whole speeches with no more alteration than was necessary to the numbers of his verse. To transcribe them into the margin was unnecessary, because the original is easily examined, and they are seldom less perspicuous in the poet than in the historian.

To play histories, or to exhibit a succession of events by action and dialogue, was a common entertainment among our rude ancestors upon great festivities. The parish clerks once performed at Clerkenwell a play which lasted three days, containing *The History of the World*.

King Lear

IV. vi. 12. *Edgar*. How fearful / And dizzy 'tis to cast one's eyes so low!] This description has been much admired since the time of Addison, who has remarked, with a poor attempt at pleasantry, that "he who can read it without being giddy has a very good head or a very bad one." The description is certainly not mean, but I am far from thinking it wrought to the utmost excellence of poetry. He that looks from a precipice finds himself assailed by one great and dreadful image of irresistible destruction. But this overwhelming idea is dissipated and enfeebled from the instant that the mind can restore itself to the observation of particulars and diffuse its attention to distinct objects. The enumeration of the choughs and crows, the samphire-man, and the fishers, counteracts the great effect of the prospect, as it peoples the desert of intermediate vacuity and stops the mind in the rapidity of its descent through emptiness and horror.

[Boswell reports an extended conversation on the same passage in *Lear*, between Johnson and several theatrical friends, under the date of October 16, 1769. In the following excerpt illustrative quotations from Congreve's *Mourning Bride* and *Lear* are inserted within double brackets.

Johnson said that the description of the temple in *The Mourning Bride* was the finest poetical passage he had ever read; he recollected none in Shakespeare equal to it.

[[*Almeria*. It was a fancied noise; for all is hushed.
Leonora. It bore the accent of a human voice.
Almeria. It was thy fear; or else some transient wind
Whistling through hollows of this vaulted aisle.
We'll listen.
Leonora. Hark!
Almeria. No, all is hushed and still as Death—'Tis dreadful!
How reverend is the face of this tall pile,

Whose ancient pillars rear their marble heads,
To bear aloft its arched and ponderous roof
By its own weight, made steadfast and immovable,
Looking tranquillity. It strikes an awe
And terror on my aching sight; the tombs
And monumental caves of death look cold
And shoot a chillness to my trembling heart.
Give my thy hand and speak to me, nay, speak,
And let me hear thy voice;
My own affrights me with its echoes.
—William Congreve, *The Mourning Bride* (1697), II. i]]

"But," said Garrick, all alarmed for "the god of his idolatry," "we know not the extent and variety of his powers. We are to suppose there are such passages in his works. Shakspeare must not suffer from the badness of our memories." Johnson, diverted by this enthusiastic jealousy, went on with great ardor: "No, Sir, Congreve has *nature*." Smiling on the tragic eagerness of Garrick, but composing himself, he added, "Sir, this is not comparing Congreve on the whole with Shakspeare on the whole; but only maintaining that Congreve has one finer passage than any that can be found in Shakspeare. Sir, a man may have no more than ten guineas in the world, but he may have those ten guineas in one piece; and so may have a finer piece than a man who has ten thousand pounds; but then he has only one ten-guinea piece. What I mean is that you can show me no passage where there is simply a description of material objects, without any intermixture of moral notions, which produces such an effect." Mr. Murphy mentioned Shakspeare's description of the night before the battle of Agincourt; but it was observed it had *men* in it. Mr. Davies suggested the speech of Juliet, in which she figures herself awakening in the tomb of her ancestors. Some one mentioned the description of Dover Cliff.

[[How fearful
And dizzy 'tis to cast one's eyes so low!
The crows and choughs that wing the midway air
Show scarce so gross as beetles; half way down
Hangs one that gathers samphire, dreadful trade!
Methinks he seems no bigger than his head.
The fishermen that walk upon the beach
Appear like mice, and yond tall anchoring bark
Diminish'd to her cock, her cock a buoy
Almost too small for sight. The murmuring surge,
That on the unnumber'd idle pebbles chafes,

Cannot be heard so high. I'll look no more,
Lest my brain turn, and the deficient sight
Topple down headlong.—*King Lear,* IV. vi. 12–25]]

JOHNSON. "No, Sir, it should be all precipice—all vacuum. The crows impede your fall. The diminished appearance of the boats and other circumstances are all very good description; but do not impress the mind at once with the horrible idea of immense height. The impression is divided; you pass on by computation, from one stage of the tremendous space to another. Had the girl in *The Mourning Bride* said she could not cast her shoe to the top of one of the pillars in the temple, it would not have aided the idea, but weakened it."] [1]

General Observation. The tragedy of *Lear* is deservedly celebrated among the dramas of Shakespeare. There is perhaps no play which keeps the attention so strongly fixed; which so much agitates our passions and interests our curiosity. The artful involutions of distinct interests, the striking opposition of contrary characters, the sudden changes of fortune, and the quick succession of events, fill the mind with a perpetual tumult of indignation, pity, and hope. There is no scene which does not contribute to the aggravation of the distress or conduct of the action, and scarce a line which does not conduce to the progress of the scene. So powerful is the current of the poet's imagination that the mind which once ventures within it is hurried irresistibly along.

On the seeming improbability of Lear's conduct it may be observed that he is represented according to the histories at that time vulgarly received as true. And perhaps if we turn our thoughts upon the barbarity and ignorance of the age to which this story is referred, it will appear not so unlikely as while we estimate Lear's manners by our own. Such preference of one daughter to another, or resignation of dominion on such conditions, would be yet credible if told of a petty prince of Guinea or Madagascar. Shakespeare, indeed, by the mention of his earls and dukes, has given us the idea of times more civilized and of life regulated by softer manners; and the truth

---

[1] Boswell reports the following opinion of Johnson's under the date of October 16, 1769: "In the description of night in *Macbeth* [III. ii] the beetle and the bats detract from the general idea of darkness—inspissated gloom."

is that though he so nicely discriminates and so minutely describes the characters of men, he commonly neglects and confounds the characters of ages, by mingling customs ancient and modern, English and foreign.

My learned friend Mr. Warton, who has in the *Adventurer* very minutely criticized this play, remarks that the instances of cruelty are too savage and shocking, and that the intervention of Edmund destroys the simplicity of the story. These objections may, I think, be answered by repeating that the cruelty of the daughters is an historical fact, to which the poet has added little, having only drawn it into a series by dialogue and action. But I am not able to apologize with equal plausibility for the extrusion of Gloucester's eyes, which seems an act too horrid to be endured in dramatic exhibition, and such as must always compel the mind to relieve its distress by incredulity. Yet let it be remembered that our author well knew what would please the audience for which he wrote.

The injury done by Edmund to the simplicity of the action is abundantly recompensed by the addition of variety, by the art with which he is made to co-operate with the chief design, and the opportunity which he gives the poet of combining perfidy with perfidy and connecting the wicked son with the wicked daughters, to impress this important moral, that villainy is never at a stop, that crimes lead to crimes and at last terminate in ruin.

But though this moral be incidentally enforced, Shakespeare has suffered the virtue of Cordelia to perish in a just cause, contrary to the natural ideas of justice, to the hope of the reader, and, what is yet more strange, to the faith of chronicles. Yet this conduct is justified by the Spectator, who blames Tate for giving Cordelia success and happiness in his alteration and declares that, in his opinion, *the tragedy has lost half its beauty*. Dennis has remarked, whether justly or not, that to secure the favorable reception of *Cato, the town was poisoned with much false and abominable criticism,* and that endeavors had been used to discredit and decry poetical justice. A play in which the wicked prosper and the virtuous miscarry may doubtless be good, because it is a just representation of the common events of human life; but since all reasonable beings naturally love justice, I cannot easily be persuaded that the observation of justice makes a play worse;

or that, if other excellencies are equal, the audience will
not always rise better pleased from the final triumph of
persecuted virtue.

In the present case the public has decided. Cordelia,
from the time of Tate, has always retired with victory and
felicity. And, if my sensations could add anything to the
general suffrage, I might relate, I was many years ago so
shocked by Cordelia's death that I know not whether I
ever endured to read again the last scenes of the play till
I undertook to revise them as an editor.

There is another controversy among the critics concerning this play. It is disputed whether the predominant
image in Lear's disordered mind be the loss of his kingdom
or the cruelty of his daughters. Mr. Murphy, a very judicious critic, has evinced by induction of particular passages that the cruelty of his daughters is the primary source
of his distress, and that the loss of royalty affects him only
as a secondary and subordinate evil. He observes with
great justness that Lear would move our compassion but
little, did we not rather consider the injured father than
the degraded king.

The story of this play, except the episode of Edmund,
which is derived, I think, from Sidney, is taken originally
from Geoffrey of Monmouth, whom Holinshed generally
copied; but perhaps immediately from an old historical
ballad, of which I shall insert the greater part. My reason
for believing that the play was posterior to the ballad,
rather than the ballad to the play, is that the ballad has
nothing of Shakespeare's nocturnal tempest, which is too
striking to have been omitted, and that it follows the chronicle; it has the rudiments of the play but none of its amplifications; it first hinted Lear's madness but did not array
it in circumstances. The writer of the ballad added something to the history, which is a proof that he would have
added more if more had occurred to his mind, and more
must have occurred if he had seen Shakespeare. [At the end
of this note Johnson appends "A Lamentable Song of the
Death of King Lear and his Three Daughters."]

Timon of Athens

IV. ii. *Enter* Flavius.] Nothing contributes more to the ex-
altation of Timon's character than the zeal and fidelity of

his servants. Nothing but real virtue can be honored by domestics; nothing but impartial kindness can gain affection from dependents.

IV. iii. 486. *Timon.* all / I kept were knaves, to serve in meat to villains.] *Knave* is here in the compounded sense of a *servant* and a *rascal*.

General Observation. The play of *Timon* is a domestic tragedy and therefore strongly fastens on the attention of the reader. In the plan there is not much art, but the incidents are natural, and the characters various and exact. The castastrophe affords a very powerful warning against that ostentatious liberality which scatters bounty but confers no benefits, and buys flattery but no friendship.

In this tragedy are many passages perplexed, obscure, and probably corrupt, which I have endeavored to rectify or explain, with due diligence; but, having only one copy, cannot promise myself that my endeavors will be much applauded.

Macbeth

Most of the notes which the present editor has subjoined to this play were published by him in a small pamphlet in 1745.

I. i. *Enter three* Witches.] In order to make a true estimate of the abilities and merit of a writer, it is always necessary to examine the genius of his age and the opinions of his contemporaries. A poet who should now make the whole action of his tragedy depend upon enchantment and produce the chief events by the assistance of supernatural agents, would be censured as transgressing the bounds of probability, be banished from the theater to the nursery, and condemned to write fairy tales instead of tragedies; but a survey of the notions that prevailed at the time when this play was written will prove that Shakespeare was in no danger of such censures, since he only turned the system that was then universally admitted to his advantage and was far from overburdening the credulity of his audience.

The reality of witchcraft or enchantment, which, though not strictly the same, are confounded in this play, has in all ages and countries been credited by the common people, and in most, by the learned themselves. These phantoms have indeed appeared more frequently in proportion as the darkness of ignorance has been more gross; but it cannot be shown that the brightest gleams of knowledge have at any time been sufficient to drive them out of the world. The time in which this kind of credulity was at its height seems to have been that of the holy war, in which the Christians imputed all their defeats to enchantments or diabolical opposition, as they ascribed their success to the assistance of their military saints; and the learned Dr. Warburton appears to believe (*Supplement to the Introduction to "Don Quixote"*) [1] that the first accounts of enchantments were brought into this part of the world by those who returned from their eastern expeditions. But there is always some distance between the birth and maturity of folly as of wickedness; this opinion had long existed, though perhaps application of it had in no foregoing age been so frequent, nor the reception so general. Olympiodorus, in Photius's extracts, tells us of one Libanius, who practiced this kind of military magic and having promised χωρὶς ὁπλιτῶν κατὰ βαρβάρων ἐνεργεῖν, *to perform great things against the barbarians without soldiers,* was, at the instances of the empress Placidia, put to death, when he was about to have given proof of his abilities. The empress showed some kindness in her anger by cutting him off at a time so convenient for his reputation.

But a more remarkable proof of the antiquity of this notion may be found in St. Chrysostom's book *de Sacerdotio,* which exhibits a scene of enchantments not exceeded by any romance of the Middle Age: he supposes a spectator overlooking a field of battle attended by one that points out all the various objects of horror, the engines of destruction, and the arts of slaughter. Δεικνύτο δὲ ἔτι παρὰ τοῖς ἐναντίοις καὶ πετομένους ἵππους διά τινος μαγγανείας, καὶ ὁπλίτας δι᾽ ἀέρος φερομένους, καὶ πάσην γοητείας δύναμιν καὶ ἰδέαν. "Let him then proceed to show him in the opposite armies horses flying by enchantment, armed men transported through the air, and every power and form of magic." Whether St. Chrysostom believed that such performances

[1] Warburton's "Supplement to the Translator's Preface" in the 1749 edition of Charles Jervas's translation of *Don Quixote* apparently bore the title "Dissertation on the Origin of the Books of Chivalry" in the first edition of 1742.

were really to be seen in a day of battle, or only endeavored to enliven his description by adopting the notions of
the vulgar, it is equally certain that such notions were in
his time received, and that therefore they were not im-
ported from the Saracens in a later age; the wars with the
Saracens, however, gave occasion to their propagation,
not only as bigotry naturally discovers prodigies, but as
the scene of action was removed to a great distance.

The Reformation did not immediately arrive at its me-
ridian, and though day was gradually increasing upon us,
the goblins of witchcraft still continued to hover in the twi-
light. In the time of Queen Elizabeth was the remarkable
trial of the witches of Warbois, whose conviction is still
commemorated in an annual sermon at Huntingdon. But
in the reign of King James, in which this tragedy was written, many circumstances concurred to propagate and con-
firm this opinion. The king, who was much celebrated for
his knowledge, had, before his arrival in England, not only
examined in person a woman accused of witchcraft but
had given a very formal account of the practices and illu-
sions of evil spirits, the compacts of witches, the cere-
monies used by them, the manner of detecting them, and
the justice of punishing them, in his dialogues of *Daemonologie,* written in the Scottish dialect, and published at
Edinburgh. This book was, soon after his accession, reprinted at London, and as the ready way to gain King
James's favor was to flatter his speculations, the system of
Daemonologie was immediately adopted by all who desired either to gain preferment or not to lose it. Thus the
doctrine of witchcraft was very powerfully inculcated; and
as the greatest part of mankind have no other reason for
their opinions than that they are in fashion, it cannot be
doubted but this persuasion made a rapid progress, since
vanity and credulity co-operated in its favor. The infec-
tion soon reached the Parliament, who, in the first year
of King James, made a law, by which it was enacted,
Chapter xii: That "if any person shall use any invocation or
conjuration of any evil or wicked spirit; 2. or shall consult, covenant with, entertain, employ, feed or reward any
evil or cursed spirit to or for any intent or purpose; 3. or
take up any dead man, woman or child out of the grave,
—or the skin, bone, or any part of the dead person, to be
employed or used in any manner of witchcraft, sorcery,

charm, or enchantment; 4. or shall use, practice, or exercise any sort of witchcraft, sorcery, charm, or enchantment; 5. whereby any person shall be destroyed, killed, wasted, consumed, pined, or lamed in any part of the body; 6. that every such person being convicted shall suffer death." This law was repealed in our own time.[1]

Thus, in the time of Shakespeare, was the doctrine of witchcraft at once established by law and by the fashion, and it became not only unpolite, but criminal, to doubt it; and as prodigies are always seen in proportion as they are expected, witches were every day discovered and multiplied so fast in some places that Bishop Hall mentions a village in Lancashire where their number was greater than that of the houses. The Jesuits and sectaries took advantage of this universal error and endeavored to promote the interest of their parties by pretended cures of persons afflicted by evil spirits; but they were detected and exposed by the clergy of the Established Church.

Upon this general infatuation Shakespeare might be easily allowed to found a play, especially since he has followed with great exactness such histories as were then thought true; nor can it be doubted that the scenes of enchantment, however they may now be ridiculed, were both by himself and his audience thought awful and affecting.

I. vii. 28. *Enter* Lady Macbeth.] The arguments by which Lady Macbeth persuades her husband to commit the murder afford a proof of Shakespeare's knowledge of human nature. She urges the excellence and dignity of courage, a glittering idea which has dazzled mankind from age to age and animated sometimes the housebreaker and sometimes the conqueror; but this sophism Macbeth has forever destroyed, by distinguishing true from false fortitude, in a line and a half; of which it may almost be said that they ought to bestow immortality on the author, though all his other productions had been lost;

> I dare do all that may become a man,
> Who dares do more, is none.

This topic, which has been always employed with too much success, is used in this scene with peculiar propriety, to

[1] This sentence was added in 1765. See Johnson's defense of the belief in witches during a conversation with Boswell, April 9, 1772.

a soldier by a woman. Courage is the distinguishing virtue
of a soldier, and the reproach of cowardice cannot be borne
by any man from a woman, without great impatience.

She then urges the oaths by which he had bound himself to murder Duncan, another art of sophistry by which
men have sometimes deluded their consciences and persuaded themselves that what would be criminal in others
is virtuous in them; this argument Shakespeare, whose
plan obliged him to make Macbeth yield, has not confuted, though he might easily have shown that a former
obligation could not be vacated by a latter; that obligations laid on us by a higher power could not be overruled
by obligations which we lay upon ourselves.[1]

II. i. 49. *Macbeth*. Now o'er the one half-world / Nature
seems dead.] That is, *over our hemisphere all action and
motion seem to have ceased.*   This image, which is perhaps the most striking that poetry can produce, has been
adopted by Dryden in his *Conquest of Mexico:*

> All things are hush'd as Nature's self lay dead,
> The mountains seem to nod their drowsy head;
> The little birds in dreams their songs repeat,
> And sleeping flow'rs beneath the night dews sweat.
> Even lust and envy sleep!

These lines, though so well known, I have transcribed,
that the contrast between them and this passage of
Shakespeare may be more accurately observed.

Night is described by two great poets, but one describes
a night of quiet, the other of perturbation. In the night of
Dryden, all the disturbers of the world are laid asleep; in
that of Shakespeare, nothing but sorcery, lust, and murder is awake. He that reads Dryden finds himself lulled
with serenity and disposed to solitude and contemplation.
He that peruses Shakespeare looks round alarmed and
starts to find himself alone. One is the night of a lover, the
other, of a murderer.

II. ii. 57. *Lady Macbeth*. gild the faces of the grooms
withal; / For it must seem their guilt] Could Shakespeare
possibly mean to play upon the similitude of *gild* and
guilt? [2]

---

[1] The last clause is added in 1765.
[2] This note is added to those of 1745 in 1765.

II. iii. 118. *Macbeth.* Here lay Duncan, / His silver skin
lac'd with his golden blood.] Mr. Pope has endeavored to
improve one of these lines by substituting *gory blood* for
golden blood; but it may easily be admitted that he who
could on such occasion talk of *lacing the silver skin* would
lace it with *golden blood.* No amendment can be made to
this line, of which every word is equally faulty, but by a
general blot.

It is not improbable that Shakespeare put these forced
and unnatural metaphors into the mouth of Macbeth as a
mark of artifice and dissimulation, to show the difference
between the studied language of hypocrisy and the natural outcries of sudden passion. This whole speech so considered is a remarkable instance of judgment, as it consists entirely of antithesis and metaphor.

III. i. 56. *Macbeth.* as it is said, / Mark Antony's was by
Caesar] Though I would not often assume the critic's privilege of being confident where certainty cannot be obtained, nor indulge myself too far in departing from the
established reading, yet I cannot but propose the rejection
of this passage, which I believe was an insertion of some
player, that, having so much learning as to discover to
what Shakespeare alluded, was not willing that his audience should be less knowing than himself and has therefore weakened the author's sense by the intrusion of a
remote and useless image into a speech bursting from a
man wholly possessed with his own present condition and
therefore not at leisure to explain his own allusions to himself. If these words are taken away, by which not only the
thought but the numbers are injured, the lines of Shakespeare close together without any traces of a breach.

My genius is rebuk'd. He chid the sisters.

This note was written before I was fully acquainted
with Shakespeare's manner, and I do not now think it of
much weight; for though the words, which I was once willing to eject, seem interpolated, I believe they may still be
genuine, and added by the author in his revision. The
author of the *Revisal* cannot admit the measure to be
faulty. There is only one foot, he says, put for another. This
is one of the effects of literature in minds not naturally
perspicacious. Every boy or girl finds the meter imperfect,

but the pedant comes to its defense with a tribrachys or an anapest and sets it right at once by applying to one language the rules of another. If we may be allowed to change feet, like the old comic writers, it will not be easy to write a line not metrical. To hint this once is sufficient.[1]

General Observation. This play is deservedly celebrated for the propriety of its fictions, and solemnity, grandeur, and variety of its action; but it has no nice discriminations of character, the events are too great to admit the influence of particular dispositions, and the course of the action necessarily determines the conduct of the agents.

The danger of ambition is well described; and I know not whether it may not be said in defense of some parts which now seem improbable, that, in Shakespeare's time, it was necessary to warn credulity against vain and illusive predictions.

The passions are directed to their true end. Lady Macbeth is merely detested; and though the courage of Macbeth preserves some esteem, yet every reader rejoices at his fall.[2]

Coriolanus

General Observation. The tragedy of *Coriolanus* is one of the most amusing of our author's performances. The old man's merriment in Menenius; the lofty lady's dignity in Volumnia; the bridal modesty in Virgilia; the patrician and military haughtiness in Coriolanus; the plebeian malignity and tribunitian insolence in Brutus and Sicinius, make a very pleasing and interesting variety; and the various revolutions of the hero's fortune fill the mind with anxious curiosity. There is, perhaps, too much bustle in the first act and too little in the last.

Julius Caesar

General Observation. Of this tragedy many particular passages deserve regard, and the contention and reconcile-

[1] This paragraph is added in 1773.
[2] This note is added in 1765.

ment of Brutus and Cassius is universally celebrated; but I
have never been strongly agitated in perusing it and think
it somewhat cold and unaffecting compared with some
other of Shakespeare's plays; his adherence to the real
story and to Roman manners seems to have impeded the
natural vigor of his genius.

Antony and Cleopatra

I. i. 10. *Philo*. gypsy's lust] *Gypsy* is here used both in the
original meaning for an *Egyptian* and in its accidental
sense for a *bad woman*.

IV. ix. 15. *Enobarbus*.

> throw my heart
> Against the flint and hardness of my fault,
> Which, being dried with grief, will break to powder,
> And finish all foul thoughts]

The pathetic of Shakespeare too often ends in the ridiculous. It is painful to find the gloomy dignity of this noble
scene destroyed by the intrusion of a conceit so far-
fetched and unaffecting.

V. ii. 4. *Cleopatra*.

> it is great
> To do that thing that ends all other deeds,
> Which shackles accidents, and bolts up change,
> Which sleeps, and never palates more the dung,
> The beggar's nurse and Caesar's.]

[Warburton had added a line and changed "dung" to
"dug."] I cannot perceive the loss of a whole line or the
need of an emendation. The commentator seems to have
entangled his own ideas; his supposition that *suicide* is
called *the beggar's nurse and Caesar's,* and his concession
that the position is *intelligible,* show, I think, a mind not
intent on the business before it. The difficulty of this passage, if any difficulty there be, arises only from this, that
the act of suicide and the state which is the effect of suicide
are confounded. Voluntary death, says she, is an act *which
bolts up change;* it produces a state,

> Which sleeps, and never palates more the dung,
> The beggar's nurse, and Caesar's.

Which has no longer need of the gross and terrene suste-
nance, in the use of which Caesar and the beggar are on a
level.

The speech is abrupt, but perturbation in such a state is
surely natural. [The First Folio reads "dung." Modern
editors incline to accept Warburton's emendation.]

General Observation. This play keeps curiosity always
busy and the passions always interested. The continual
hurry of the action, the variety of incidents, and the quick
succession of one personage to another, call the mind forward without intermission from the first act to the last.
But the power of delighting is derived principally from the
frequent changes of the scene; for, except the feminine
arts, some of which are too low, which distinguish Cleopatra, no character is very strongly discriminated. Upton,
who did not easily miss what he desired to find, has discovered that the language of Antony is, with great skill
and learning, made pompous and superb, according to his
real practice. But I think his diction not distinguishable
from that of others; the most tumid speech in the play is
that which Caesar makes to Octavia.

The events, of which the principal are described according to history, are produced without any art of connection
or care of disposition.

Cymbeline

III. v. 71. *Cloten.*

>   And that she hath all courtly parts more exquisite
>   Than lady, ladies, woman; from every one
>   The best she hath]

["The second line is intolerable nonsense. It should be read
and pointed thus,

>   Than lady ladies; *winning* from each one." Warburton.]

I cannot perceive the second line to be intolerable, or to
be nonsense. The speaker only rises in his ideas. *She has all
courtly parts,* says he, *more exquisite than* any *lady,* than
all *ladies,* than all *womankind.* Is this nonsense?

V. i. 1–33. *Posthumus.* Yea, bloody cloth, I'll keep thee.]

This is a soliloquy of nature, uttered when the effervescence of a mind agitated and perturbed spontaneously and inadvertently discharges itself in words. The speech, throughout all its tenor, if the last conceit be excepted, seems to issue warm from the heart. He first condemns his own violence; then tries to disburden himself by imputing part of the crime to Pisanio; he next soothes his mind to an artificial and momentary tranquillity by trying to think that he has been only an instrument of the gods for the happiness of Imogen. He is now grown reasonable enough to determine that having done so much evil he will do no more; that he will not fight against the country which he has already injured; but as life is not longer supportable, he will die in a just cause and die with the obscurity of a man who does not think himself worthy to be remembered.

General Observation. This play has many just sentiments, some natural dialogues, and some pleasing scenes, but they are obtained at the expense of much incongruity.

To remark the folly of the fiction, the absurdity of the conduct, the confusion of the names and manners of different times, and the impossibility of the events in any system of life, were to waste criticism upon unresisting imbecility, upon faults too evident for detection, and too gross for aggravation.

Troilus and Cressida

General Observation. This play is more correctly written than most of Shakespeare's compositions, but it is not one of those in which either the extent of his views or elevation of his fancy is fully displayed. As the story abounded with materials, he has exerted little invention; but he has diversified his characters with great variety and preserved them with great exactness. His vicious characters sometimes disgust but cannot corrupt, for both Cressida and Pandarus are detested and contemned. The comic characters seem to have been the favorites of the writer; they are of the superficial kind and exhibit more of manners than nature; but they are copiously filled and powerfully impressed.

Shakespeare has in his story followed, for the greater

part, the old book of Caxton, which was then very popular; but the character of Thersites, of which it makes no
mention, is a proof that this play was written after Chap-
man had published his version of *Homer*.

Romeo and Juliet

II. iv. 138. *Mercutio*. No hare, sir] Mercutio having
roared out, *So ho!*, the cry of the sportsmen when they
start a hare, Romeo asks *what he has found*. And Mercutio answers, *No hare*, &c. The rest is a series of quibbles
unworthy of explanation, which he who does not understand needs not lament his ignorance.

III. v. 86. *Juliet*.

>   Ay, madam, from the reach of these my hands.
>   Would none but I might venge my cousin's
>   death!]

Juliet's equivocations are rather too artful for a mind disturbed by the loss of a new lover.

General Observation. This play is one of the most pleasing of our author's performances. The scenes are busy
and various, the incidents numerous and important, the
catastrophe irresistibly affecting, and the process of the
action carried on with such probability, at least with such
congruity to popular opinions, as tragedy requires.

Here is one of the few attempts of Shakespeare to exhibit the conversation of gentlemen, to represent the airy
sprightliness of juvenile elegance. Mr. Dryden mentions a
tradition, which might easily reach his time, of a declara-
tion made by Shakespeare, that *he was obliged to kill
Mercutio in the third act, lest he should have been killed
by him.* Yet he thinks him *no such formidable person but
that he might have lived through the play and died in his
bed,* without danger to a poet. Dryden well knew, had he
been in quest of truth, that in a pointed sentence more regard is commonly had to the words than the thought, and
that it is very seldom to be rigorously understood. Mercutio's wit, gaiety, and courage will always procure him
friends that wish him a longer life; but his death is not
precipitated, he has lived out the time allotted him in the

construction of the play; nor do I doubt the ability of
Shakespeare to have continued his existence, though some
of his sallies were perhaps out of the reach of Dryden,
whose genius was not very fertile of merriment nor
ductile to humor, but acute, argumentative, comprehensive, and sublime.

The nurse is one of the characters in which the author
delighted; he has, with great subtilty of distinction, drawn
her at once loquacious and secret, obsequious and insolent,
trusty and dishonest.

His comic scenes are happily wrought, but his pathetic
strains are always polluted with some unexpected depravations. His persons, however distressed, *have a conceit
left them in their misery, a miserable conceit.*

Hamlet

II. ii. 86–167. *Polonius.* My liege, and madam, to expostu-
late] [Warburton believed that Polonius should be inter-
preted as a "weak, pedant, minister of state," a satire on
Elizabethan courtly rhetoric and stock moralizing.] This
account of the character of Polonius, though it sufficiently
reconciles the seeming inconsistency of so much wisdom
with so much folly, does not perhaps correspond exactly
to the ideas of our author. The commentator makes the
character of Polonius a character only of manners, discriminated by properties superficial, accidental, and ac-
quired. The poet intended a nobler delineation of a mixed
character of manners and of nature. Polonius is a man
bred in courts, exercised in business, stored with observations, confident of his knowledge, proud of his eloquence,
and declining into dotage. His mode of oratory is truly
represented as designed to ridicule the practice of those
times, of prefaces that made no introduction, and of
method that embarrassed rather than explained. This part
of his character is accidental, the rest is natural. Such a
man is positive and confident, because he knows that his
mind was once strong and knows not that it is become
weak. Such a man excels in general principles but fails in
the particular application. He is knowing in retrospect
and ignorant in foresight. While he depends upon his memory and can draw from his repositories of knowledge, he

utters weighty sentences and gives useful counsel; but as
the mind in its enfeebled state cannot be kept long busy
and intent, the old man is subject to sudden dereliction
of his faculties, he loses the order of his ideas and en-
tangles himself in his own thoughts, till he recovers the
leading principle and falls again into his former train. This
idea of dotage encroaching upon wisdom will solve all the
phenomena of the character of Polonius.

III. i. 59. *Hamlet.* Or to take arms against a sea of trou-
bles] [For "against a sea" Warburton had suggested
"against assail."] Mr. Pope proposed *siege.* I know not why
there should be so much solicitude about this metaphor.
Shakespeare breaks his metaphors often, and in this desultory speech there was less need of preserving them.

III. ii. 138. *Hamlet.* Nay, then, let the devil wear black, for
I'll have a suit of sables.] I know not why our editors
should, with such implacable anger, persecute our predecessors. Οἱ νεκροὶ μὴ δάκνουσιν. The dead, it is true, can
make no resistance, they may be attacked with great security; but since they can neither feel nor mend, the safety of
mauling them seems greater than the pleasure; nor perhaps
would it much misbeseem us to remember, amidst our
triumphs over the *nonsensical* and the *senseless,* that we
likewise are men; that *debemur morti,* and, as Swift observed to Burnet, shall soon be among the dead ourselves.

I cannot find how the common reading is nonsense, nor
why Hamlet, when he laid aside his dress of mourning, in
a country where it was *bitter cold,* and the air was *nipping
and eager,* should not have a *suit of sables.* I suppose it is
well enough known that the fur of sables is not black.

III. iii. 94. *Hamlet.* his soul may be as damn'd and black /
As hell, whereto it goes.] This speech, in which Hamlet,
represented as a virtuous character, is not content with
taking blood for blood, but contrives damnation for the
man he would punish, is too horrible to be read or to be
uttered.

IV. v. 84. *King.* In hugger-mugger to inter him] All the
modern editions that I have consulted give it,

                   In private to inter him.

That the words now replaced are better, I do not undertake to prove; it is sufficient that they are Shakespeare's. If phraseology is to be changed as words grow uncouth by disuse or gross by vulgarity, the history of every language will be lost; we shall no longer have the words of any author; and, as these alterations will be often unskillfully made, we shall in time have very little of his meaning.

General Observation. If the dramas of Shakespeare were to be characterized each by the particular excellence which distinguishes it from the rest, we must allow to the tragedy of *Hamlet* the praise of variety. The incidents are so numerous that the argument of the play would make a long tale. The scenes are interchangeably diversified with merriment and solemnity; with merriment that includes judicious and instructive observations, and solemnity not strained by poetical violence above the natural sentiments of man. New characters appear from time to time in continual succession, exhibiting various forms of life and particular modes of conversation. The pretended madness of Hamlet causes much mirth, the mournful distraction of Ophelia fills the heart with tenderness, and every personage produces the effect intended, from the apparition that in the first act chills the blood with horror to the fop in the last that exposes affectation to just contempt.

The conduct is perhaps not wholly secure against objections. The action is indeed for the most part in continual progression, but there are some scenes which neither forward nor retard it. Of the feigned madness of Hamlet there appears no adequate cause, for he does nothing which he might not have done with the reputation of sanity. He plays the madman most when he treats Ophelia with so much rudeness, which seems to be useless and wanton cruelty.

Hamlet is, through the whole play, rather an instrument than an agent. After he has, by the stratagem of the play, convicted the king, he makes no attempt to punish him, and his death is at last effected by an incident which Hamlet has no part in producing.

The catastrophe is not very happily produced; the exchange of weapons is rather an expedient of necessity than a stroke of art. A scheme might easily have been formed to kill Hamlet with the dagger, and Laertes with the bowl.

The poet is accused of having shown little regard to poetical justice and may be charged with equal neglect of poetical probability. The apparition left the regions of the dead to little purpose; the revenge which he demands is not obtained but by the death of him that was required to take it; and the gratification which would arise from the destruction of an usurper and a murderer is abated by the untimely death of Ophelia, the young, the beautiful, the harmless, and the pious.

Othello

I. iii. 140–170. *Othello*. Wherein of antres vast and deserts idle] Whoever ridicules this account of the progress of love shows his ignorance, not only of history, but of nature and manners. It is no wonder that, in any age, or in any nation, a lady, recluse, timorous, and delicate, should desire to hear of events and scenes which she could never see and should admire the man who had endured dangers and performed actions which, however great, were yet magnified by her timidity. [For "deserts idle" Pope had suggested "deserts wild."] Every mind is liable to absence and inadvertency, else Pope could never have rejected a word so poetically beautiful.

III. iii. 90. *Othello*. Excellent wretch! Perdition catch my soul / But I do love thee!] The meaning of the word *wretch* is not generally understood. It is now, in some parts of England, a term of softest and fondest tenderness. It expresses the utmost degree of amiableness, joined with an idea, which perhaps all tenderness includes, of feebleness, softness, and want of protection. Othello, considering Desdemona as excelling in beauty and virtue, soft and timorous by her sex, and by her situation absolutely in his power, calls her *excellent wretch!* It may be expressed,

> Dear, harmless, helpless excellence.

III. iv. 102. *Emilia*. 'Tis not a year or two shows us a man.] From this line it may be conjectured that the author intended the action of this play to be considered as longer than is marked by any note of time. Since their arrival at Cyprus, to which they were hurried on their wedding night, the fable seems to have been in one continual progress, nor can I see any vacuity into which a *year or two,* or even a month or two, could be put. On the night of Othello's arrival, a feast was proclaimed; at that feast Cassio was degraded, and immediately applies to Desdemona to get him restored. Iago indeed advises Othello to hold him off awhile, but there is no reason to think that he has been held off long. A little longer interval would increase the probability of the story, though it might violate the rules of the drama.

V. ii. 20. *Othello.*

> I must weep,
> But they are cruel tears; this sorrow's heavenly,
> It strikes where it doth love. She wakes.]

This tenderness, with which I lament the punishment which justice compels me to inflict, is a holy passion.

I wish these two lines could be honestly ejected. It is the fate of Shakespeare to counteract his own pathos.

[Boswell reports the following under the date of April 12, 1776.

I observed the great defect of the tragedy of *Othello* was that it had not a moral; for that no man could resist the circumstances of suspicion which were artfully suggested to Othello's mind. JOHNSON. "In the first place, Sir, we learn from *Othello* this very useful moral, not to make an unequal match; in the second place, we learn not to yield too readily to suspicion. The handkerchief is merely a trick, though a very pretty trick; but there are no other circumstances of reasonable suspicion, except what is related by Iago of Cassio's warm expressions concerning Desdemona in his sleep; and that depended entirely upon the assertion of one man. No, Sir, I think *Othello* has more moral than almost any play."]

General Observation. The beauties of this play impress themselves so strongly upon the attention of the reader that they can draw no aid from critical illustration. The fiery openness of Othello, magnanimous, artless, and credulous, boundless in his confidence, ardent in his affection, inflexible in his resolution, and obdurate in his revenge; the cool malignity of Iago, silent in his resentment, subtle in his designs, and studious at once of his interest and his vengeance; the soft simplicity of Desdemona, confident of

merit and conscious of innocence, her artless perseverance
in her suit, and her slowness to suspect that she can be suspected, are such proofs of Shakespeare's skill in human
nature as, I suppose, it is vain to seek in any modern
writer. The gradual progress which Iago makes in the
Moor's conviction and the circumstances which he employs to enflame him are so artfully natural that, though
it will perhaps not be said of him, as he says of himself,
that he is *a man not easily jealous,* yet we cannot but pity
him when at last we find him *perplexed in the extreme.*

There is always danger lest wickedness, conjoined with
abilities, should steal upon esteem, though it misses of approbation; but the character of Iago is so conducted that
he is from the first scene to the last hated and despised.

Even the inferior characters of this play would be very
conspicuous in any other piece, not only for their justness
but their strength. Cassio is brave, benevolent, and honest,
ruined only by his want of stubbornness to resist an in-
sidious invitation. Roderigo's suspicious credulity and im-
patient submission to the cheats which he sees practiced
upon him, and which by persuasion he suffers to be repeated, exhibit a strong picture of a weak mind betrayed
by unlawful desires to a false friend; and the virtue
of Emilia is such as we often find, worn loosely but not
cast off, easy to commit small crimes but quickened and
alarmed at atrocious villainies.

The scenes from the beginning to the end are busy,
varied by happy interchanges, and regularly presenting
the progression of the story; and the narrative in the end,
though it tells but what is known already, yet is necessary to produce the death of Othello.

Had the scene opened in Cyprus, and the preceding incidents been occasionally related, there had been little
wanting to a drama of the most exact and scrupulous reg-
ularity.

DRAMABOOKS

Hill and Wang has established DRAMABOOKS as a permanent library of the great classics of the theatre of all countries, in an attractive, low-priced format.

PLAYS

MD 1   *Christopher Marlowe* edited by Havelock Ellis. Introduction by John Addington Symonds (Tamburlaine the Great, Parts I & II, Doctor Faustus, The Jew of Malta, Edward the Second)

MD 2   *William Congreve* edited by Alexander Charles Ewald. Introduction by Macaulay (Complete Plays)

MD 3   *Webster and Tourneur* Introduction by John Addington Symonds (The White Devil, The Duchess of Malfi, The Atheist's Tragedy, The Revenger's Tragedy)

MD 4   *John Ford* edited by Havelock Ellis (The Lover's Melancholy, 'Tis Pity She's a Whore, The Broken Heart, Love's Sacrifice, Perkin Warbeck)

MD 5   *Richard Brinsley Sheridan* edited with an Introduction by Louis Kronenberger (The Rivals, St. Patrick's Day, The Duenna, A Trip to Scarborough, The School for Scandal, The Critic)

MD 6   *Camille and Other Plays* edited, with an Introduction to the well-made play by Stephen S. Stanton (Scribe: A Peculiar Position, and The Glass of Water; Sardou: A Scrap of Paper; Dumas, *fils*: Camille; Augier: Olympe's Marriage)

MD 7   *John Dryden* edited, and with an Introduction by George Saintsbury (The Conquest of Granada, Parts I & II, Marriage à la Mode, Aureng-Zebe)

MD 8   *Ben Jonson* edited, with an Introduction and Notes, by Brinsley Nicholson and C. H. Herford (Volpone, Epicoene, The Alchemist)

MD 9   *Oliver Goldsmith* edited by George Pierce Baker with an Introduction by Austin Dobson (The Good Natur'd Man, She Stoops to Conquer, An Essay on the Theatre, A Register of Scotch Marriages)

MD 10   *Jean Anouilh* Volume 1 (Antigone, Eurydice, The Rehearsal, Romeo and Jeannette, The Ermine)

MD 11   *Let's Get a Divorce! and Other Plays,* edited, and with an Introduction on The Psychology of Farce by Eric Bentley (Labiche: A Trip Abroad, and Célimare; Sardou: Let's Get a Divorce!; Courteline, These Cornfields; Feydeau: Keep an Eye on Amélie; Prévert: A United Family; Achard: essay on Feydeau)

MD 12   *Jean Giraudoux* adapted and with an Introduction by Maurice Valency (Ondine, The Enchanted, The Madwoman of Chaillot, The Apollo of Bellac)

MD 13   *Jean Anouilh* Volume 2 (Restless Heart, Time Remembered, Ardèle, Mademoiselle Colombe, The Lark)

MD 14   *Henrik Ibsen: The Last Plays* Introduction and translation by William Archer (Little Eyolf, John Gabriel Borkman, When We Dead Awaken)

MD 15   *Ivan Turgenev* translated by Constance Garnett (A Month in the Country, A Provincial Lady, A Poor Gentleman)